Portraits of Brockport's Past

Portraits of Brockport's Past

True Tales About the Victorian Village on the Erie Canal

William G. Andrews

America Through Time®
ADDING COLOR TO AMERICAN HISTORY

This book is dedicated to the many local historians, listed in the Introduction, on whose shoulders I have stood.

America Through Time is an imprint of Fonthill Media LLC
www.through-time.com
office@through-time.com

Published by Arcadia Publishing by arrangement with Fonthill Media LLC
For all general information, please contact Arcadia Publishing:
Telephone: 843-853-2070
Fax: 843-853-0044
E-mail: sales@arcadiapublishing.com
For customer service and orders:
Toll-Free 1-888-313-2665

www.arcadiapublishing.com

First published 2019

ISBN 978-1-63499-178-0

Typeset in 10.5pt on 13pt Sabon
Printed and bound in England

Contents

INTRODUCTION

The purpose of this book is to present brief essays on nearly 100 topics relevant to the history of a small canal town in western New York. The illustrations have not appeared in my earlier books. Over half of the essays are biographical sketches of some of the families, men, and women who created the history recounted on these pages. After all, history does not just happen—men and women are the forces that make it happen. Most of them were factors in the history of the village, but a surprisingly large number left Brockport and made their marks in the wider world outside, and some did both. The essays all concern events and people in the history of the village before the outbreak of World War II, except for a small amount of spillover to the post-World War II period. Brockporters were involved in the three wars during the period covered and some of the essays deal with those experiences.

My son, Bill, Jr., provided invaluable technical support and Sue Savard, chief volunteer at the Emily L. Knapp Museum and Rozenn Bailleul-LeSuer, Historian of the Western Monroe Historical Society, helped immensely in locating suitable illustrations. In addition, I am grateful for Brockport's many, devoted local historians on whose work I have freely drawn. Besides Sue and Rozenn, they include Sarah Cedeno, Eunice Chesnut, James Cornes, Charlie Cowling, Wayne Dedman, Harold and Helen Dobson, Merritt Elwell, Alicia Fink, Gordon and Peg Fox, Mary Jo Gigliotti, Kathy Goetz, David Hale, Leanna Hale, Carol Hannan, Wilbur "Doc" Hiler, Shirley Husted, Hazel Kleinbach, Norm and Emily Knapp, Ed Lehman, W. Bruce Leslie, Charlotte Martin, Jackie Morris, Kenneth O'Brien, Mary Smith, Ray Tuttle, and Scott Warthman.

1

Notable Brockport Families

The Seymours

The Seymours were, probably, Brockport's most distinguished family in the nineteenth century, from the time James partnered with Hiel Brockway in laying out the village in 1822 until William's death in 1903 at the age of 101. Horatio Seymour, a first cousin of James and William, was a Civil War governor of New York and Democratic candidate for U.S. President in 1868. Another first cousin was on the New York State Canal Commission while the canal was under construction. Eight Seymours have been members of the U.S. Congress. Richard, the first of the American Seymours, arrived in Connecticut in 1639. The following paragraphs will look at the Seymours who were important in Brockport's history.

James Seymour

James Seymour is less well known in Brockport than his partner, Hiel Brockway, because he left the village rather early, while Brockway lived here the rest of his life and was important in the life of the village. While Seymour's role as co-founder of the village is well known, less well known is his very distinguished career apart from that.

James was born in Litchfield, Conn., in 1791, and moved to Murray Four Corners, now Clarkson Corners, in 1817, where he established a dry goods and grocery store. He was active in politics as a town supervisor. After founding and moving to Brockport, he was the town's first postmaster and was Sweden Town supervisor in 1824–25. He also operated two grain warehouses and was a partner in a canal line boat company. However, James's land speculations in Brockport proved unprofitable. He and his partners liquidated their holdings.

While living in Brockport, he was a leader in the effort for the creation of Monroe County and, in 1821, when that was accomplished, was appointed Monroe County's first sheriff. In 1825, he was elected to a three-year term. In 1826, he moved to Rochester and continued his business and political career. He was the first cashier and, later, the president of the first bank in Rochester, vice-president of the first railroad to reach Rochester, and first treasurer of the Rochester Athenaeum (now the Rochester Institute of Technology). He was also a city alderman and a leader of the county Jacksonian party.

In 1836, Seymour bought 18,000 acres of land in Michigan and, in 1847, moved there. With his brother, Charles, he was a founder of the Town of Flushing and was its first settler. He became the supervisor of the Town of Lansing. He served in both houses of the state legislature, was one of the founders of the Republican Party in Michigan, and was involved in founding the national Republican Party.

In 1847, the Michigan state legislature struggled with relocating the state capital. It was located at that time in Detroit, which was viewed as being too vulnerable to an attack from Canada. Almost every town in Michigan vied for the honor. The Senate voted fifty-two times in an effort to settle the issue. The House of Representatives had already decided on thirteen other towns.

Seymour campaigned for Lansing, although it was almost uninhabited. He paid the state $15,000, donated 20 acres of land, and signed a contract with the state to "erect on his land ... a good and substantial wood or brick building or buildings ... suitable for the sessions of the legislature and Supreme Court, for the Governor and State Library and for offices for the Auditor General, State Treasurer, Adjutant General, and Clerk of the Supreme Court." He was to lease them without charge until a permanent building was erected there.

Also, Seymour offered to donate 206 acres for building lots, built a dam on the Grand River, a bridge across it, a hotel to accommodate state legislators, and helped finance construction of a plank road linking Lansing to Detroit.

In a history of Genesee County, Michigan, he is described as "one of the ablest men in the state." He died in 1864 at the age of seventy-three. He had nine children. Among their descendants were John Foster Dulles, Secretary of State, and Allen Dulles, CIA Director, both under Eisenhower.

William Henry Seymour

William Henry Seymour, younger brother of James, the co-founder of Brockport, was born in Litchfield, Conn., in 1802. He joined his brother at his store in Murray Four Corners in 1818 and moved with him to Brockport in 1822. When James relocated to Rochester in 1826, William took over the store and succeeded him as postmaster.

William was very active politically. He was an ardent Jacksonian, one of the three members of the Central Committee of the local party and one of its delegates to

Monroe County conventions of Republican Young Men. In 1832, he was elected a village trustee and he also served on the board of health.

In the early 1830s, he made his first foray into the foundry business as a partner in the Backus & Ganson foundry, which manufactured threshing machines. I have an 1842 dunning letter signed BackusSeymour, suggesting to me that he was a partner in the firm that became Backus & Fitch. In 1844, he persuaded twenty-five-year-old Dayton Morgan to join him in founding the Globe Iron Works (which became Seymour & Morgan) to manufacture stoves and agricultural implements.

A year later, Cyrus McCormick came to Brockport and hired the firm of (now) Backus & Fitch to manufacture 100 of his reapers. The result was a failure; either they did not produce the machines or the reapers did not work. In any case, McCormick then hired Seymour & Morgan to produce 100 reapers and they worked, inaugurating the Industrial Revolution in agriculture.

Seymour sold his patent rights to Morgan in 1857 and retired from the firm in 1877 and it was reorganized as D. S. Morgan & Co. He then went into business with his son, Henry, who had moved to Sault Ste. Marie, Mich., in 1873. Henry shipped timber to his father, who operated a lumber mill in Brockport.

In 1836, William married Narcissa ("Nancy") Pixley, who had come to Brockport in 1820 to become the first school mistress in the village. She was the niece of Peletiah Rogers, an early merchant and a relative of the Seymours. In 1823, Rogers had built the house at 49 State Street that now houses the Village Court. He had built it in the style of a Dutch row house, much like the Presbyterian manse that was demolished long ago. Upon his marriage, William bought the Rogers home and lived there the rest of his long life. He remodeled it extensively, giving it a very different appearance. In the 1860s, he added the mansard roof.

After retiring from business in 1882, Seymour continued to lead an active life. He traveled to Europe on a five-week trip at the age of eighty-one and again at the age of eighty-six. At ninety-two years, he spent most of the summer in Chicago, visiting the Columbian Exhibition nearly every day. At the age of 100, the whole village celebrated his birthday and he took an automobile ride. He remained in good health until three weeks before his death in October 1903 at age 101.

Henry William Seymour

Henry William Seymour also had a distinguished career. He was born in Brockport in 1834, the son of William. He attended Brockport schools, the Brockport Collegiate Institute, the Canandaigua Academy, Williams College, and Albany Law School and passed the bar in May 1856, but never practiced law. In 1852, he opened a factory manufacturing reapers, rotary pumps, and engines, directly across the street from his father's reaper factory.

Henry was also active in local politics, serving three terms on the village board in the late 1860s. He and Thomas Cornes were the most active advocates in the campaign to secure the normal school for the village and he served on its board. Early in the Civil War, he was active in recruiting efforts in the village but, though the very eligible age of twenty-six, never entered the armed forces.

In 1873, he moved to Sault Ste. Marie, Michigan, where he built a sawmill and planing mill, farmed, and resumed manufacturing reapers and other farm implements. He was vice-president of the First National Bank, president of St. Mary's Water-Power Co., and shipped timber to his father.

He was a very busy man in Michigan, for he pursued political as well as business interests. He served in the state House of Representatives (1880–82) and the state Senate (1882–84 and 1886–88). In February 1888, he was elected as a Republican to an unexpired term in the U.S. House of Representatives, but served only until March 1889. He was an unsuccessful candidate for re-election in 1888, losing in the primaries. He died on a trip to Washington in 1906.

The Dobsons

Thomas Hopper Dobson

Thomas Hopper Dobson was a prominent fixture on Brockport's business scene for fifty-four years. He was also a civic leader. He was born in Vienna, Oneida County, on January 11, 1852. He came to Brockport in 1876 and bought the drugstore of Timothy Frye. In 1901, he bought the druggist business of Joseph A. Tozier and moved across Main Street to No. 56. One legacy of the business was the series of some 137 postcards from the early twentieth century that it published.

Dobson was village president (mayor) in 1895 and a trustee in 1887 and 1905. He also served on the water commission and was a member of the board of the Normal School, becoming secretary when Daniel Holmes died in 1919. He was a charter member of the Lake View Cemetery Association and its longtime secretary. He was a leader in St. Luke's Episcopal Church as a senior warden and a fifty-seven-year member of the Masonic Lodge.

Thomas died in December 1930.

Harold Gardner Dobson

Harold Gardner Dobson, Thomas's son, joined the firm in 1906 and carried on the business after his father's death. He was born in Brockport in 1886 and studied at the Brockport Normal School and earned a pharmacy degree from the University of Buffalo in 1906. He was also a director and president of the Ellicott Drug Co., a large wholesale firm in Buffalo.

Harold followed in his father's footstep at St. Luke's as vestryman, warden, and treasurer. He was the local correspondent for several Rochester and Buffalo newspapers and the Western Union Telegraph agent. He was a charter member of the Kiwanis Club and secretary of the Silsby Hose Co. He was also the executive secretary of the Monroe County Agricultural Society while its fair was in Brockport. He was a member of the Monroe County Republican Committee and a charter member of the Monroe County Planning Board. He was an unsuccessful candidate for mayor. He was a very active member of the Masonic Lodge, holding many offices over the years. He and his wife, Helen, were the official village historians.

Harold was succeeded upon his death in 1965 by his daughter-in-law, Ruth Stock Dobson, and her brother-in-law, Edwin Kewin. The store finally closed in 1967.

The Gordons

The Gordons were a distinguished Brockport business and political family. Luther was an exceptionally versatile, enterprising, and successful businessman. He was born in Rushford, NY, in 1822 and entered the business world at the age of nineteen as owner of a foundry furnace and the inventor of a plow that he manufactured. He sold that business after a year and a half and pursued the mercantile trade for fourteen years, erecting two buildings to house his two general stores. Meanwhile, he was a livestock broker for sixteen years and entered the lumber business.

In 1856, Luther bought a lumberyard in Brockport and built a steam sawmill and planing mill. He purchased several hundred acres of timber land in Cattaraugus County and 7,000 acres in Michigan. Eventually, he had sawmill operations in East Saginaw and Sterling, Mich., and Holley and Olean, NY, and shipped lumber and finished lumber (sashes, doors, ornamental trim, etc.) throughout the East. In the early 1870s, he expanded his lumber business by building several canal boats.

In 1863, he founded the First National Bank of Brockport as its president. Also, he was in the construction business. Most notably, he built his own home across South Street from the Morgan-Manning house, the First National Bank building on the corner of Main and King Streets, the homes that are now the Roxbury and the Webster Funeral Home, the houses along Gordon Street, and the First Baptist Church.

Luther was also prominent in the community's political life, serving as village mayor in 1861 and 1872 and town supervisor in 1868. He died in March 1881. He succeeded in the foundry, mercantile, livestock, lumber, planing, construction, and banking businesses and was a civic leader—quite a record.

George was the only child of Luther and his wife, Florilla. He became his father's business partner and succeeded him. Besides the lumber business and the First National Bank, George was president of the Brockport Building & Loan Assn. and trustee of the Fidelity Trust Company in Buffalo. He and his wife, Ida, had five sons, four of whom survived childhood. Luther, George, Jr., and Thomas followed their father as bankers. They demolished Luther Sr.'s 1873 bank building and erected the present structure in 1927. The lumber business and the bank failed in the early years of the Great Depression of the 1930s. The manager of the lumber business, W. E. B. Stull, however, continued in that trade by establishing Stull Lumber and Hardware on Park Avenue, now owned and managed by his grandson, Bill.

George and Ida Gordon owned a five-bedroom cottage on 3 acres of land in the then-thriving lakeside resort of Troutberg. They had a tennis court, a large picnic house, and a boathouse for two boats. The arrival of the Gordons was a major event in Troutberg, as described in Mary Smith's *Remembering Hamlin* book: "Old timers fondly recalled the sight and sound of the Gordon tally-ho, with the uniformed driver of four horses up front and the footman at the rear, sounding blasts on his bugle." That was also a familiar sight in the village, as described by Ray Tuttle: the Gordon's carriage, "passing through the streets, loaded with guests, and tended by bright uniformed coachmen, footmen, and accompanied by a bugler provided one of the thrills for the pedestrians of that day." I believe that the Gordons's tally-ho is now above the fireplace in the dining room of the Morgan-Manning house.

Thomas became president of the First National Bank, serving until it was closed after President Roosevelt's Bank Holiday of 1933. He and his wife, Ruth, lived very opulent lives with nannies for their children, a cook, a maid, a chauffeur, gardeners, and a carpenter. Dinner, as described by Thomas's son in one of Eunice Chesnut's books, included finger bowls, imported lace tablecloths, and sparkling polished silver. Thomas owned three automobiles, including a limousine. Their estate on the corner of North Main Street and West Avenue included greenhouses where Thomas pursued his horticultural hobby. They later became Rogers Florists. In 1934, he was convicted of having deceived the bank examiners and was fined $5,000.

George, Jr., was vice-president of the bank and president of the Brockport Piano Co. Fred married an heiress, was a gentleman farmer, and built Whitehall, the nine-bedroom mansion in Clarkson that was recently the home of the Sagawa family.

Quite a family—through three generations.

The Clevelands

Merritt A. Cleveland

Merritt A. Cleveland was born in 1849, the son of a Jefferson County farmer. He began his career as a civil engineer in 1870 at the age of twenty-one, and already by 1872 was in charge of constructing the Lake Ontario Shore Railroad. His later projects included building part of the Canadian Pacific Railroad in Canada's Northwest, major portions of the Welland and Murray canals in Canada, the Toronto harbor, and the north channel of the St. Lawrence River.

Other railroads that he built were the Pittsburgh, Cleveland, and Toledo Railroad in Pennsylvania and Ohio, which became part of the Baltimore and Ohio system, and the Kingston & Pembroke Railroad in Canada.

Merritt and his family, including five-year-old Milo, moved to Brockport in 1884. In 1888, he had the contract for paving Brockport's Main Street. He built the large white clapboard house on the southeast corner of Adams and Allen Streets and Milo built the house just east of the former Newman Oratory. Milo attended Brockport schools and the Brockport Normal School.

Merritt's last project was constructing the Town of Sweden section of the New York State Barge Canal and the locks at Waterford in 1912. He died on May 23, 1912, before those projects were completed.

Milo Cleveland

Milo Cleveland took over the company after his father's death, completed his projects, and, in 1913–14, built the locks, dams, and bridge on the Seneca River. I have been unable to learn if the company continued after that. Milo served as vice-president of the First National Bank until its failure in 1933. While he was the bank's vice-president, he defeated Thomas Gordon, the bank's president, for village trustee, fifty-seven votes to fifty-five. He served until 1922, but did not seek re-election, nor did Thomas Gordon. Milo died in 1954.

The Harmons

Austin Harmon

Austin Harmon was born in Rupert, Vermont, in 1809 and trained in the marble business there. In 1828, he came to Brockport by packet boat before Brockport was even incorporated as a village and opened a monument store on Main Street. In 1869, he moved his shop to Market Street.

From his arrival here, Austin was active in civic affairs. Already by 1831, he was a leader in the youth temperance organization, one of the most important civic movements of the time. By 1840, still only thirty-one years old, he became a village trustee and later he served as Justice of the Peace for fifteen years. Also, he was a major in the militia, an important post at the time.

George Harmon, Sr.

George Harmon, Sr., Austin's son, was born in 1842. He graduated from the Brockport Collegiate Institute. In 1885, Austin retired and George succeeded him in the marble business. At the same time, George bought an insurance agency and continued both businesses for the rest of his life.

George, Sr., continued his father's tradition of civic activity. He was secretary of the Agricultural Society that organized the county fair annually, one of the founders and secretary of the New York State Association of Town Fairs, and treasurer of the Brockport Businessmen's Assn. He was also a member of the Board of the Brockport

Normal School. In 1889, he was appointed Brockport's postmaster, a patronage appointment under Republican President Benjamin Harrison. He remained in that post until his death in 1910.

George Harmon, Jr.

George Harmon, Jr., George Sr.'s son, born in 1880, served out his father's term as postmaster until 1912, when Democrat Woodrow Wilson became president. Also, he was Town of Sweden clerk in 1905, 1908–10, and 1913–14, and a director of the First National Bank. He was elected village mayor in 1914 and served throughout World War I until 1920, the longest tenure in the history of the office until that time. Under his administration, Main Street was paved and our water system installed. Remarkably, he returned to the mayoralty twenty-five years later in 1939 and served through World War II until 1946. He was also a trustee of both the Lakeview and High Street cemeteries.

George, Jr., had two sons. One became a professor at Princeton and the other was an attorney.

All three Harmons were leaders in the Republican town committee and both Georges were trustees of Brockport's business organization, the Board of Trade in 1907. George, Jr., continued in the insurance business until his death in the early 1960s. Thus, three generations of Harmons were leaders in the business, political, and civic life of this community over a span of more than 130 years.

The Seldens

Henry Roger Selden

Henry Roger Selden was Clarkson's most distinguished resident. Residing there from 1830 until 1859. He had been born in North Lyme, Conn., in 1805. He read law with his older brother, Samuel, in Rochester in 1825 and began to practice law in Clarkson in 1830.

From 1847 until 1853, Selden and his wife owned a house on Mechanci Street (now Park Avenue) in Brockport and from 1839 to 1855, they owned the block of land in Brockport bounded on the south by College Street, on the west by Utica Street, on the north by Monroe Avenue, and on the east by Main Street.

In 1854, Selden played a major role in the organization of the Republican Party in New York State and was elected lieutenant governor in 1856. He was a supporter of William Seward at the Republican National Convention in 1860, but, nevertheless, was offered the vice-presidential nomination by Abraham Lincoln. He declined on grounds of ill health and recommended Hannibal Hamlin, who was nominated and elected.

In 1862, he was appointed Chief Judge of the N.Y.S. Court of Appeals, the highest state court, but deferred to the longest-serving associate judge. In 1863, he was elected to an associate judgeship, but resigned in 1865 because of ill health. He was elected to the N.Y.S. Assembly in 1865.

Selden was an ardent abolitionist and supporter of women's suffrage. After John Brown's raid at Harper's Ferry, a warrant was issued for the arrest of Rochester resident Frederick Douglass. Selden learned of this by chance and alerted Douglass, enabling him to escape to Canada and on to England. He was also the chief counsel for Susan B. Anthony after her arrest for voting illegally in the 1872 election and posted bail for her when she was to be incarcerated—over her objections.

Selden was also the first president of a telegraph company that became part of Western Union. After the merger, he was a board member and counsel for Western Union. Finally, he was a serious legal scholar, publishing at least two treatises on aspects of the law. He died in 1885.

George Baldwin Selden

George Baldwin Selden, Henry's son, was born in Clarkson in 1846. When he was a lad of fourteen, he was influenced to undertake his life's work by overhearing a conversation between his father and Dayton Morgan while walking with them from Brockport to Clarkson. The two men agreed that self-propelled vehicles for public roads were impractical. That inspired George to undertake a decades-long effort to invent a means of mechanical propulsion for such a vehicle.

As a youth and young man, he spent every available moment working on his invention. While in grammar school in Clarkson, he would frequent metal-working shops to get ideas. He was sent to a prep school in Vermont, but dropped out because he was spending more time in a local machine shop than in class

When the Civil War broke out, he enlisted in the 6th U.S. Cavalry Regiment, but his father arranged his discharge on grounds of poor eyesight. He then joined a hospital unit. After the war, he entered a business in Virginia to mine soapstone, but that failed and he returned to Clarkson. He then enrolled in the University of Rochester, but transferred to Yale and studied law. Although he preferred studying a technical subject, he managed to finish and passed the bar in 1871.

While at Yale, his father was stricken with a throat ailment that required surgery in Vienna. Selden accompanied his father there. Upon his return, he joined his father's law practice. One of his clients was George Eastman. Still restless, he went to work in a barrel hoop factory in Chicago. While there, he invented a machine for manufacturing hoops for skirts. He also invented a typewriter. However, the factory burned in the Great Chicago Fire of 1871 and he returned to Rochester.

He now opened a law practice specializing in patent law, but also undertook serious efforts to build a practical automobile engine. He worked in a small work shop in Rochester experimenting with engines propelled by steam, ammonia gas, bisulphide of carbon (a mixture of "laughing gas" and kerosene), and other liquid fuels. In 1875, he went bankrupt trying to build a six-cylinder engine, but received financial support from Hiram Everest of the Vacuum Oil Company.

In 1876, he visited the Philadelphia World's Fair and saw a gasoline-powered internal combustion engine invented by George Brayton. It was immense, much too large to propel an automobile. His great achievement was to reduce the size of gasoline engines to the point that they were a practical means of propelling a vehicle. By 1878, he had a 400-pound one-cylinder engine.

By 1879, Selden produced a prototype and submitted a patent application. However, he did not mount the engine on a vehicle. He offered his invention to large manufacturing firms, but none were interested. As a skilled patent attorney, he kept revising his patent application, thus prolonging its validity, until it acquired commercial value. His patent was finally granted in 1895. In 1900, the Hartford Electric Vehicle Co. of Hartford, Conn., purchased his patent. In 1904, he finally built a vehicle and mounted his engine on it.

Meanwhile, the Winton Co. of Cleveland began building automobiles using Selden's patent. He sued successfully for patent infringement and Winton began paying royalties. Other manufacturers then got on board and formed the Association of Licensed Automobile Manufacturers that paid royalties to Selden. For the years 1903–05, he received royalties amounting to $360,000.

A group of auto manufacturers, led by Henry Ford, refused to pay the royalty and were sued by Selden and his associates. After eight years of litigation, Ford and his associates prevailed. However, Selden was not done with the automobile business. In 1906, he formed the Selden Motor Vehicle Co. with his two sons. In 1912, they created a subsidiary to manufacture trucks. It thrived, absorbed the parent company, and survived until 1930. In the meantime, Selden had died in 1922.

The Holmeses

Elias Bellows Holmes

Elias Bellows Holmes was a leader in transportation, politics, business, education, agriculture, and the law. He had been born in Fletcher, Vt., on May 22, 1807, the son of Joseph (d. 1825) and Diantha Bellows Holmes (d. 1824) and attended St. Albans Academy.

His childhood was difficult, as both of his parents had died by the time he was aged eighteen and he was left the sole support for three younger siblings. He did farm labor in the summer and taught school during the winter. At the age of twenty, he moved to Pittsford, NY, to study law with his mother's brother, Judge Ira Bellows. He was admitted to the bar in 1830 and came to Brockport to practice law in 1831. In 1835, he married Maria Brockway, daughter of Hiel Brockway, co-founder of Brockport. They had three children: Mary (1836–1873), Edgar (b. 1838), and Ira (1840–1895).

Elias was elected to the U.S. House of Representatives as a Whig in 1844 and re-elected in 1846. He did not run for re-election in 1848. He opposed the Mexican War and the annexation of Texas and spoke out against the extension of slavery into the territories, but opposed abolitionism and was content to leave slavery alone in the states where it already existed. A History of Congress said that "his annual income exceeds that of any other member of the present Congress."

Elias's endeavors in transportation included a line of packet boats that ran from Rochester to Buffalo from 1840 to 1855 in competition with the Red Bird line of his father-in-law, Hiel Brockway. Later, he was one of the promoters and constructors and a director of the Rochester & Niagara Falls Railroad, which still serves Brockport, and a director of the New York Central and Hudson Valley Railroad after the two merged. He helped start the Toledo & Wabash railroads.

While he was in Congress, he rendered an invaluable service to the village by persuading Cyrus McCormick to come to Brockport to arrange for his reaper to be manufactured. For many years in the 1850s and 1860s, he was a leader of the Republican Party in Brockport and Monroe County and campaigned actively for Lincoln in the 1860 and 1864 elections, including being a Monroe County delegate to the N.Y.S. Union (Republican) convention.

In business, he was the founding president of the Brockport Gas Co., vice-president and trustee of the Brockport Savings Bank, and owner of a hotel where the Brockport United Methodist Church is located now. His real estate had the highest valuation in the village in 1850. Also, he bought and sold homes, vacant lots, and farms as a business and owned a flour mill in Hamlin. He was probably Brockport's wealthiest resident.

In education, he was a trustee of the Brockport Collegiate Institute and one of its most active promoters. He was the principal speaker at its 1862 commencement ceremony.

His first love seems to have been agriculture. He owned and operated farms, including the largest farm in the Town of Sweden. He bred Black Hawks, a beautiful breed of light carriage horses. He was a leader in agricultural organizations. He was the founding and perennial president of the Brockport Union Agricultural Society, which sponsored the annual county fair. He was also the most successful prize winner at those fairs, including for horses, cows, and even cheese. He was president of both the Monroe County and New York State Agricultural Societies and one of the organizers of the Western New York Agricultural Society.

During the Civil War, he was Brockport's most prominent patriot. He led recruiting efforts, presiding at war meetings and giving long speeches, not only in Brockport but in neighboring towns as well. He was the most generous contributor, by far, to relief efforts for soldiers and their families. For instance, he donated $1,000 in the first drive to raise money for the families of soldiers, twice as much as any other contributor and he organized and led the Union Mite Society, which raised money for soldiers' relief.

At his death, he was president of the Brockport Gas Light Co., a director of the Third National Bank of Chicago, and a trustee of the Brockport Collegiate Institute. He died in 1866, aged fifty-nine, and is buried in the High Street cemetery.

Ira Holmes

Ira Holmes, Elias's son, was a student at the University of Rochester at the outbreak of the Civil War. He was commissioned a second lieutenant in the 3rd New York Cavalry regiment in August 1862 and was promoted to captain as a result of his recruiting efforts. However, he served for only six months. On returning to Brockport, he entered the banking business. By 1870, he was in the banking and real estate business in Chicago and was, apparently, quite successful, for he was living on Michigan Avenue—the "Gold Coast"—with real estate worth $100,000 and personal property of equal value. By 1880, he and his wife had two sons, a daughter, and five servants.

Elias Burton Holmes

Elias Burton Holmes, one of Ira's sons, became wealthy as a well-known photographer, filmmaker, and traveler. He coined the term "travelogue" and was the first travel lecturer to incorporate photo slides and movies into his performances. Over the course of his career, he delivered 8,000 travel lectures. He and his wife had a fourteen-room apartment on Fifth Avenue in New York with 20-foot ceilings. It was filled with treasures from his many trips that he sold to "Believe-it-or-not" Ripley. Because he produced travel films for Hollywood studios, he also had a twelve-room "bungalow" in California. One of his biographers called him "the greatest traveler of his time."

He attended the first Olympic Games and rode in the first train on the Trans-Siberian Railroad. The George Eastman House in Rochester has twenty reels of his travel films. He died in 1958.

The Daileys

William Dailey, Sr.

William Dailey, Sr., was a prominent Brockport businessman for many years and sired a large family of entrepreneurs and leaders of the N.Y.S. Democratic Party. His parents had both emigrated from Ireland during the potato famine years of the 1840s. He was born on the family farm near Scottsville on April 14, 1846. In 1865, he founded a produce business on the canal in Brockport and rapidly became the leading produce dealer in western New York. In 1880, he moved his business to the railroad at Park Avenue. He dealt in wheat, wool, beans, wood, coal, cabbage, potatoes, apples, and general produce of all kinds.

He also had large elevators in Brockport and Medina. They shipped over a thousand carloads of stock annually.

A big part of his business was supplying all of the wheat for the shredded wheat cereal business in Niagara Falls.

Dailey was heavily involved in other commercial enterprises in Brockport. He was a director of the Moore-Shafer Shoe Mfg. Co., the Brockport Cold Storage Co., the Brockport Piano Co., the Rochester Wheel Co., and the State Bank of Commerce. He was an ardent Democrat, but never sought public office

Dailey built one of the finest homes in Brockport at 52 South Avenue, with a slate roof and redwood siding. His sons, William and Franklin, inherited the house. Many years later, it stood empty and, finally, in the 1990s, was seized and demolished by the village; the property became a park and playground.

He and his wife, the former Jessie McGary, had nine sons and one daughter. Most of the sons followed their father into the produce business in one way or another.

John F. Dailey, Sr.

John F. Dailey, Sr., William's son, became the manager of his father's business in 1892. In 1897, he became a full partner, and in 1905, he bought the business. John, Sr., also invested in an unsuccessful three-wheeled car and owned liquor stores in Buffalo and Rochester and an orange juice dairy and sandwich shop in Buffalo. He branched out from the produce business, investing in an invention that would teach a person how to drive a golf ball.

In the early years of the twentieth century, he was a delegate to every N.Y.S. Democratic convention and, in 1904, to its national convention. He was a village trustee, 1902–04, and an unsuccessful candidate for mayor in 1904.

William Dailey, Jr.

William Dailey, Jr., another of William Sr.'s sons, took over the Brockport business from his brother in 1902 and moved the company to Rochester. He claimed to be the most extensive dealer in New York State in wheat and barley, with elevators all over the state and customers throughout the United States. William, Jr., also had a produce business in Albion and a beer distributorship and was a director of the Rochester Wheel Co.

John F. Dailey, Jr., and Murray Dailey, John Sr.'s sons, became New York State Amateur Golf champions.

Philip Dailey

Philip Dailey, another son of John, Sr., operated the Albion Produce Co. with Murray. Philip had also been executive secretary of the Rochester Democratic Committee and Murray had been Democratic chairman of Orleans County. Still another son became a lawyer in N.Y.C. and another was an architect in Arizona.

Franklin Dailey

Franklin Dailey followed his older brothers in running the Brockport firm until it went bankrupt in the late 1920s. The George Terry produce business later occupied the premises until they burned in a chemical fire in 1989.

Oswald Dailey

Oswald Dailey had a miniature golf course in Brockport with his brother, Franklin. He was a high civil servant in President Franklin Roosevelt's Federal Housing Administration.

One or another of the Dailey brothers had branches of their businesses in Albion, Morton, Oakfield, and Kendall.

Donald Dailey

Donald Dailey, still another brother, had a coal yard on the Park Avenue property. Later, he moved to Rochester and was Rochester Postmaster, 1941–53, Commissioner of Public Safety, and was prominent in philanthropic and civic activities. He was a delegate to the Democratic National Conventions in 1928, 1936, and 1940, and to the New York State Convention to ratify the Twenty-first Amendment to the Federal Constitution in 1933. He chaired the Monroe County Democratic Committee, 1936–40. He was also vice-president of the Genesee Brewing Co.

Vincent Dailey

Vincent Dailey, yet still another brother, was active in Democratic state politics. He was the Democrats' State Campaign Manager for the presidential, senatorial, and congressional elections of 1932–38 and a delegate to Democratic National Conventions of 1940, 1944, 1948, and 1952. He chaired the State Democratic Committee in 1938.

As political secretary to Governor Lehman in 1938, Vincent met a delegation from Brockport in his New York City office, heard their plea for survival of Brockport's State Normal School, and instructed the state budget director to include in the 1938 budget funds for the construction of a new building for the institution and, thus, its survival.

Vincent was also a businessman. He added a canning factory to the Dailey's produce business. It produced "Dailey's Old-Fashioned Jams." During World War I, "Millions of cans were bought and distributed ... by the Red Cross, Y.M.C.A., K of C., U.S. Army and the English, French and Belgian Governments." At various times, he was president of a Rhode Island knitting firm, and manager of the Duffy-Powers Department Store in Rochester. So, Brockport's Dailey family loomed large on the New York State commercial and political landscape for a long time.

The Grahams

Merritt E. Graham

Merritt E. Graham, according to the *Brockport Republic*, "was a resident of Brockport for a number of years ... and built up a large practice and made a host of warm friends" before moving to Rochester. He had graduated from the University of Michigan with a medical degree in 1878. Apparently, he entered the practice of homeopathic medicine in Brockport soon after. In 1889 and 1892, he was endorsed for County Coroner by the Union Republican Club of Brockport of which he was a member. He held the office of coroner from 1890–99. In 1900, he founded the Graham Highland Park Sanatorium and Maternity Hospital in Rochester, the predecessor of Highland Hospital. He died in 1905.

Corden T. Graham

Corden T. Graham, Merritt's son, was born in Brockport in 1881. He graduated from the Genesee Wesleyan Seminary in Lima, but did not pursue a career in the ministry. Instead, he graduated from the University of Michigan Homeopathic College with an M.D. degree and succeeded his father as head of the Sanatorium. Also, in 1903, he graduated from the National College of Electro Therapeutics. The Sanatorium's building is now an apartment house. He was married to Louise M. Williams, a Brockport resident.

The Morgans

Dayton S. Morgan

Dayton S. Morgan was one of Brockport's most distinguished and wealthiest citizens. He was born in Spencerport in 1819, the descendant of a distinguished New England family. His wife, Susan Joslyn, was a member of an equally notable New Jersey family. Dayton, Ohio, was named for one of her relatives.

Morgan's mother died soon after his birth and his father, suffering financial troubles, decamped to Ohio, leaving seventeen-year-old Dayton in the care of an aunt in Brockport. Thus Morgan was an orphan whose only resources were his talents, energy, and ambition. He graduated from the Brockport State Normal School and briefly taught school. He contemplated becoming a lawyer, but lacked the means to support himself during the long period of preparation, so he undertook a career in business.

First, he worked as a clerk in the toll collector's office in Brockport, but soon was employed by a Brockport merchant. His industry as a store clerk caught the attention of William H. Seymour who hired him in 1844 as a machinist in what was first called the Globe Iron Works and later Seymour, Chappell & Co. Morgan became the junior partner a year later, when he bought out Thomas Roby's interests. This was the firm that manufactured the first 100 successful McCormick reapers. From 1853 to 1873, George Allen was also a partner.

The firm produced reapers under McCormick's patents until 1849. Then they switched to the New Yorker model that had been invented by George Barnett, Seymour & Morgan's shop foreman.

In 1857, Seymour sold his patent rights to Morgan, who became the senior partner in the firm. They included Seymour's invention of the quadrant platform and Palmer and Williams's self-raking mechanism. Those patent rights were a major source of Morgan's wealth. For instance, Cyrus McCormick paid Seymour and, then, Morgan $60,000 in royalties from 1852 to 1872. Virtually all farm implement manufacturers paid royalties to the Brockporters.

In 1864, while living in a hotel in downtown Brockport, he married Susan Joslyn. The newlyweds rented quarters in what is now the Morgan-Manning House. Morgan bought the house in 1867 and it remained in the family until the 1964 fire.

In 1875, Seymour retired from the company and it was reorganized as D. S. Morgan & Co. Apparently, Morgan was an organizational genius. An Australian geographer called Morgan a "remarkable" manager of a far-flung industrial enterprise. At a time of serious impediments to rapid transportation and communication, Morgan managed successfully an enterprise with operations in Brockport, Philadelphia, New York, Chicago, and San Francisco. He also marketed his products and had a factory in Europe.

Morgan was also a vice-president of the New York Central Railroad, a founder of Brockport's electric company, an organizer of the Central Crosstown street railway in New York City, chair of the Board of the Brockport State Normal School, and a village trustee. Morgan owned 800 acres that is now part of the city of Chicago. He died in 1890 and left an estate reputed to amount to $2 million.

Gifford Morgan

Gifford Morgan followed in his father's footsteps as an industrialist and civic leader. He was probably Brockport's most important and influential citizen for a time. Gifford was the sixth-born child and the last of Dayton Morgan's four sons. He was born in 1873. He farmed in Clarkson and lived for a time in Buffalo, where he "had business interests."

In 1897, when he was aged twenty-four, he was a founder, vice-president, and 1906–13 president of the Rochester Wheel Co., which occupied the former Plant 2 of the D. S. Morgan and Co. farm implement factory. It manufactured wheels for wagons and carriages, but automobiles were replacing horse-drawn vehicles and the company ceased business in 1913.

A year later, the building became the Brockport Cold Storage Co. with Morgan as vice-president. It was one of the pioneer cold storage plants in the country. From

1921 until his death, he was the company president. That business was his most lasting industrial legacy as it is still a cold storage plant over a century later.

He was vice-president of the First National Bank from 1921 until it failed in 1933 and president of the Brockport National Bank that succeeded it. He was also president-treasurer of the D. S. Morgan Co., which owned the Morgan Building in Buffalo, the first steel-framed skyscraper in Buffalo that he had built with funds from Dayton Morgan's legacy.

Morgan was also a leading member of the Republican committee in Clarkson and on the executive committee of the County Committee. From 1932 until his death, he was a State GOP Committee member. He was elected town justice in 1911.

During World War I, he led the home front war effort, including head of the Sweden War Council, Food Administrator for Clarkson, chair of the Liberty Bond committee, and Fuel Administrator for Monroe County outside Rochester. He was also a sergeant in the National Guard.

Morgan was an active member and often leader of many organizations. He was one of the organizers of the Brockport Yacht Club and owner of several boats, including the *Seamaid,* a 63-foot, two-masted sailboat so large that he had to moor it at the Rochester Yacht Club. Other organizations where he played prominent roles were the Chamber of Commerce, the Red Cross chapter, the Boy Scout Council, the Masonic Lodge, the Bird Club, the Brockport Automobile Club, the Monroe County Agricultural Society, and the Silsby Hose Co. He was a member of the Normal School's Board of Trustees for more than twenty years and its president for his last nine years.

Morgan died February 3, 1944, aged seventy. His obituary in the *Brockport Republic-Democrat* called him "one of Brockport's outstanding citizens and businessmen."

2

Notable Brockport Men

Who Stayed Home

Wilson Henry Moore

Wilson Henry Moore was born in Clarkson in April 1859, the son and grandson of Clarkson farmers, and attended the Brockport State Normal School. Already as a boy, he showed business enterprise by obtaining a Kelsey hand press and printing and selling business and calling cards. In 1878, at the age of nineteen, he founded the Moore Subscription Agency based on the "clubbing" concept, whereby subscribers received discounts by ordering several magazines at once. One obituary claimed that "by means of that plan he did more than any other man to bring good reading to the homes of our land."

In 1882, he moved his company to King Street in Brockport, and when that building burned in 1888, he moved it to the vacant former office building of D. S. Morgan & Co. on Market Street. He expanded the business by buying two Chicago magazine agencies. His business was so successful that it became the world's largest subscription agency, mailing 1 million of its catalogs annually, and had 100 employees. Its business alone raised the Brockport post office from fourth class to second class and qualified the village for home mail delivery.

In 1888, he and his cousin, Manley Shafer, acquired the bankrupt Ham-Rogers Shoe factory that was housed in another former D. S. Morgan building on Market Street. They expanded it and built the brick building near the railroad on Park Avenue that burned in 1974. The shoe business thrived, producing high-end ladies' shoes for nationwide distribution and had 400 employees.

Moore was also a partner with F. F. Capen in the Brockport Piano Co. and with Gifford Morgan in the Rochester Wheel Works. He served on the Normal School

Board and was a founder of the Brockport Rural Cemetery and a vestryman at St. Luke's Episcopal Church. He owned the first automobile in Brockport.

In 1887, he married May Scranton, a Brockport woman. They had two children, Henry Wilson and Helen. When the Rochester, Lockport, Buffalo electric railway was being laid out, it was slated to pass in front of the Moore house at 39 State Street. Wilson was adamantly opposed to it. He fought it in every way he could. In 1907, he realized that he had lost the battle and went to Canada with his physician and two nurses and shot himself.

His widow sold the subscription business to the Cottrell Agency in North Cohocton and it continued as the Moore-Cottrell agency until 1974, using the clubbing concept that Moore had invented nearly a century earlier. She lived on in Brockport with her two children until her death in 1949. Helen married one of her father's employees, Stanley H. Geerer, and owned the family home until she died in 1981.

Henry was drafted in 1917 and served in the field artillery. He was an officer in the Moore-Shafer Shoe Manufacturing Co. until it failed in 1927. After that, Henry was a traveling cigar salesman.

Henry married in 1919. He and his wife, Marian, were avid and quite successful amateur golfers. They also took annual cruises to the Caribbean and South America. After Marian's death in the early 1960s, Henry and Helen lived in the same nursing home, but had become estranged and would not speak to one another. Reportedly, he had suffered from bouts of mental illness since childhood. I bought his house in 1970 and found four barrels of shoe lasts in the basement. I visited him once at the Brightonian, but he was very uncommunicative. Neither Helen nor Henry had any children.

Wilson has no descendants. All of his businesses have failed, and none of the buildings they erected still stand. Only the house he built on State Street and the flagpole he raised in front of the Moore-Shafer Shoe Co. remain as the legacy of a man who was once one of the most enterprising businessmen in Brockport history.

George F. Barnett

George F. Barnett may well be one of the great, unsung heroes as an inventor. He was born in Oneida County in 1804 and moved to Brockport in 1826. In his early life, he was an architect and carpenter. According to a contemporary source, he was employed by Cyrus McCormick from 1840 to 1845 to help him perfect his reaper. In 1845, he joined the Globe Iron Works in Brockport as plant superintendent. The firm later became Seymour & Morgan.

The basis of my belief that he was a great inventor arises from what seems to have been his role in making possible the production of successful reapers. In fourteen years, McCormick had been unable to solve the problem of manufacturing his reaper in quantity. Nor had he devised a way for the operator of his reaper to ride on the machine. Either the seat would unbalance the machine or get in the way of the reel. Those problems were solved by Seymour & Morgan, as they produced the first 100 successful reapers, which were equipped with seats for the operators.

It is unclear who in the firm actually deserves the credit for that accomplishment. It may have been a team effort, but as Barnett was in charge of that work as the plant superintendent, he was probably its principal contributor. As the reaper was the first successful farm machine, Barnett may well be credited with bringing the Industrial Revolution to the world's agriculture, one of the most important developments of the nineteenth century.

In 1850, Seymour & Morgan stopped producing the Barnett machine and he left their employ and joined George F. Whiteside in founding a rival farm implement manufacturing firm. They acquired the property where Hiel Brockway's boatyard and brickyard had burned down in 1848 and constructed the building that still exists at 60 Clinton Street. In 1886, Whiteside died, Barnett retired, and the factory closed. Their buildings later housed, in succession, a flour mill, a lumberyard, a fruit packing plant, a farm implement dealership, and an automobile repair shop.

Barnett was also active politically, first as a Whig and then as a Republican. He served as a village trustee in 1833. Religiously, he was a leading member of the Presbyterian Church. He built the house that still stands at 26 State Street. He had married in 1828 and had three children. One of his descendants, living in Florida, called me several years ago to ask about the Barnett house. Barnett died in 1897 at the age of ninety-three and is buried in the High Street cemetery.

Byron Huntley and Samuel Johnston

Byron Huntley and Samuel Johnston were the principal owners of the Brockport factory that, at one time, was the largest in Monroe County. Huntley was born in the Town of Mexico, Oswego County, in 1825, the son of a doctor of Scottish birth. He moved to Brockport with his family in 1844 and enrolled in the Brockport Collegiate Institute, but dropped out because of ill health. He later attended Madison (now Colgate) University in Hamilton, NY. He returned to Brockport as a clerk in the Backus & Fitch foundry that produced the first, unsuccessful McCormick reapers. In 1850, he became a partner in that firm, which evolved through partnership and name changes into the Johnston Harvester Co. by 1868, after Samuel Johnston became a partner and company president with Huntley as secretary-treasurer.

Samuel Johnston was born in Shelby, Orleans County, in 1835 and began a career as an inventor of agricultural machinery before the age of twenty-one. Aged twenty, he invented a planter. He patented many devices over many years, and he worked for farm implement manufacturers in Buffalo and Syracuse before coming to Brockport.

At the age of thirty, Johnston patented one of his more important inventions, a combined rake and reel. The driver of that machine could lower its cutting edge to scoop up fallen grain. This improvement earned Johnston much income in royalties from other reaper manufacturers.

Johnston was also a proficient linguist and an amateur artist who studied under Jules Marie Auguste Laroux and Jean-Paul Laurens in Paris. He helped Louis Pasteur develop a filtering device and met Count Leo Tolstoy. He was also a village trustee in 1872.

Apparently Johnston was less a business manager than an inventor for he resigned as president of Johnston Harvester Co. in 1875. He then worked with Dayton Morgan to develop the Triumph No. 2 reaper that was equipped with his rake and reel device. However, that was unsuccessful and he formed Samuel Johnston & Co. as a vehicle for his inventing, patenting, and licensing agricultural devices. His last patent was issued only days before he died. He died penniless in 1911 and is buried in Lakeview Cemetery.

The Johnston Harvester Co. occupied a factory on North Main Street. In the early 1880s, it encountered labor troubles and the factory burned in June 1882, perhaps as a result of arson. Following the fire, the company moved to Batavia, because of its location on two main rail lines, but probably also to avoid the troublesome Brockport workers.

Huntley was a businessman, not an inventor. He served as company president from 1875 until his death in 1906, but he was, above all, a salesman. His greatest feat was introducing American farm machinery to the European market, thus bringing the industrial revolution to European agriculture. He traveled to Europe annually from 1870 until he suffered a disabling stroke in 1902. He arranged for the sale of his company's products in France, Germany, Russia, Australia, and in the Middle East and Africa. For his service to French agriculture, he was decorated a Chevalier of the Legion of Honor by the French president.

Huntley was founder and sponsor of the Brockport Fire Department's Byron E. Huntley Steamer Co., which existed from 1877 until 1910.

Huntley died in 1906 and is buried in a family plot in a Cleveland, O., cemetery. He never married and had no direct survivors. His estate was estimated at $440,000 to $920,000, an enormous amount in 1906. Among the beneficiaries was the First Baptist Church of Brockport, which received $2,000. Five fire companies in Batavia received $800 each, but the Byron E. Huntley Steamer Co. received nothing.

The Johnston Harvester Co. was acquired by the Canadian farm implement manufacturer Massey-Harris in 1910 and continued in operation until 1958.

Horatio N. Beach

Horatio N. Beach is best remembered as the founder and publisher of the *Brockport Republic*, but he had a far larger impact on Brockport than that suggests. Beach was born in Greene County, New York, in 1826, but his family moved to Bridgeport, Conn., when he was a boy. His father was a merchant and Horatio succeeded to the business at his father's death in 1847.

Beach seems to have moved to Brockport in October 1856 for the purpose of founding a newspaper to support the candidacy of John C. Fremont, the first Republican presidential candidate. Local newspapers and committees were essential elements in the organization of American national political parties after the innovations by Martin Van Buren on behalf of Andrew Jackson in the late 1820s. After the Republican Party began to emerge in 1854, its leaders undertook to pull together such a network.

In his first issue, Beach announced: "Our paper will be REPUBLICAN in politics, [but] we do not intend to make politics the leading object of our paper." He retired as publisher in favor of his son, Lorenzo, in June 1871, but he remained its political editor and continued in active association with the paper until six days before his death.

He was also active in business. He organized the Brockport Businessmen's Association and was its first president. He initiated the formation of the Brockport Union Agricultural Society that ran the county fair in Brockport for many years and was its secretary. He was also founding secretary of the Brockport Electric Co. and one of the founders of the Brockport Gas Light Co., the Brockport Piano Manufacturing Co., the Moore-Shafer Shoe Manufacturing Co., and a fruit cannery. He engaged in real estate development and home building in the area of Beach Street. There was hardly a major business activity in Brockport that did not have his imprint.

He was also a mover and shaker in community affairs. He established and ran for many years Brockport's first free book lending library. He was the founding secretary of a farmer's club and secretary of two fraternal lodges. He organized the Brockport Rural Cemetery Association and spearheaded the drive to build the Soldiers' Memorial Tower. He was a toll collector for the canal and a trustee of the Brockport Collegiate Institute.

Politically, he was a village trustee and a leader of the Republican Party locally and in the county. Diplomatically, he was a United States Consul in Mexico, Venezuela, and Ecuador.

Beach died on September 21, 1896—forty years after his arrival in Brockport. Throughout that long residency here, he was a pillar of the community.

Edward C. Harrison

Edward C. Harrison, merchant tailor and clothier, was one of Brockport's leading business and civic leaders for many decades. Harrison was born in England in 1831, immigrated to the United States in 1850, came to Brockport in 1858, and established a clothing business.

Years later, he recounted his early business. In those days, he said, housewives produced homespun cloth out of which he cut the pieces for the clothing and sold the buttons and trimming, but the housewives produced the finished garments. Also, payment was usually in produce. He rarely sold socks in those days.

Later, he became a pioneer in the manufacture of ready-made clothing that he sold through outlets in the Midwest as well as in the Brockport area. At one time, he employed 200 workers in his Brockport operation. When factory-made clothing became fashionable, he reverted to strictly local business.

He continued in the business until his death at eighty-five years old, in 1916. His sixty-six years were said to have been a record for a clothing business in New York State. His son, Joseph, continued the business for another sixteen years.

Harrison was also active in civic affairs, as toll collector for the Port of Brockport for two years, village trustee for five terms, and member of the Board of the Normal School for twenty-two years. The Harrison Hose Co. of Brockport's Fire Department was named for him.

Harrison was married first in England. After that wife died in 1865, he married a woman from Hamlin. After she died in 1898, he married her sister. He had eight children.

Although the Harrison business is long gone from Brockport, he remains a presence in the community through the legacy of the home he built about 1870 at the end of College Street, the finest example of a Second Empire architectural-style residence in the village. One of his granddaughters became a successful illustrator of children's books and used her grandfather's house as a model for some of her illustrations. When his second wife died, the State Normal School bought the property and Harrison moved to the Getty House Hotel at the corner of Market and Main. When he remarried, they lived at 234 Main Street.

The College Street house became the residence for the principals of the Normal School from 1898 until 1942 and the presidents of the college until 1964. It was then used successively as offices for the college's English Department and as an "executive dining room". In 1974, the Brockport Alumni Association acquired it and spent about half a million dollars restoring it. It has become an asset for the community as a venue for special events and meetings.

Thomas Cornes

Thomas Cornes was one of Brockport's most prominent citizens, but he is largely forgotten today. He was born in England in 1813 and immigrated with his family to New York's Madison County in 1827. In 1834, he moved to Brockport, where he spent the rest of his life, living at 26 South Street.

Cornes was a butcher by trade, invested heavily in real estate, and was very active in public life. He was co-owner of the largest meat market in Brockport and owned a large complex of buildings on the east side of the village that served as a slaughterhouse. He also owned three farms, five stores on Main Street, a warehouse on the canal, a distillery, a retail plaster shop, and several dwellings. He and his son, Charles, held a patent for a refrigeration device.

Cornes probably holds Brockport's record for the number of times he was elected to municipal boards. He was elected to the village board seven times and served as its president for five of those years. He was elected Town of Sweden supervisor three times. He was frequently a delegate to various political party conventions. His political success is the more remarkable in that he was a Jeffersonian Democrat at a time that the village and town were heavily Republican. By one account, he was the leading Democrat on the west side of the county.

Cornes was appointed to political patronage jobs, canal toll collector in the 1850s and during the Civil War, and manager of the Western House of Refuge in Rochester, a home for orphaned and wayward boys.

He was also active in other civic affairs. He was on the Boards of the Brockport Collegiate Institute and the State Normal School. He shared with Henry Seymour credit for having had the greatest influence in bringing the Normal School to Brockport. He was treasurer of the Brockport Union Agricultural Society that operated the county fair. He was an active firefighter and one of the original fire companies in the village was named for him. During the Civil War, he was among the most active leaders in the various efforts to support the war.

Cornes was also very litigious. He frequently protested his property assessments, refused to pay his taxes, and intimidated the village collector. He had raucous quarrels with his neighbors over trees, sidewalks, sewers, and election bets. During one such dispute, a neighbor commented that he "never knew a case before where Mr. Cornes had nothing to say." On one occasion, he brought a number of serious charges against a canal superintendent, all of which were dismissed. He engaged in a long-running feud with Horatio Beach, publisher of the *Brockport Republic*. When things did not go his way in the Democratic Party, he supported Republicans.

Thomas Cornes died on December 20, 1878 at the age of sixty-five.

Daniel Holmes

Daniel Holmes is mostly remembered as having been the husband of Mary Jane Holmes, internationally famous as an "authoress" and active in the Brockport community's social and church life, but Daniel was a more important civic leader. He had been born in Ontario County in 1828. His father was a pioneer and proprietor of a hotel. Daniel graduated from the Brockport Collegiate Institute and Yale University and received a master's degree from the University of Rochester.

He began his career as a school teacher, but soon turned to law, passing the bar in 1852 and establishing a practice in Brockport the following year. He quickly became the leading attorney in the village. When the figures were published in 1868 and 1918, he had the highest income of any lawyer in the village. He became a judge in 1856 and served in that capacity for thirty years. He was elected village clerk in 1854 and held that office for twenty-six years.

He began his partisan political career as secretary of Brockport's Know Nothing committee, as the anti-immigrant American Party was known, but he soon became a leader in Brockport's Republican Party. At various times, he was an inspector of elections, frequent delegate to district and judicial conventions, candidate for coroner, and vice-president and secretary of its caucus. He ran unsuccessfully for village president in 1875.

Holmes was active in other civic affairs as well. He was a pillar of the Brockport Collegiate Institute and its successor, the Brockport State Normal School. He served on its Board of Trustees as the secretary for sixty-five years, adding the job of treasurer toward the end.

He also served on Brockport's Board of Health, was a director of the YMCA and the Brockport Loan & Building Association, vice-president of the Brockport Rural Cemetery Association, a founder of the National Historical Society of New York, and an officer of the Free Library and Reading Club. He sold insurance and bought and sold real estate.

In St. Luke's Episcopal Church, he served as a vestryman or warden for sixty-five years and a teacher and treasurer of the Sunday school. He was also a delegate to several diocesan conferences. He was a leader of the Masonic Lodge, and Brockport's chapter was named in his honor.

How he met all those responsibilities while traveling as exhaustively as he and Mary Jane did escapes my understanding. They vacationed two to three months every summer on Martha's Vineyard, traveled extensively in the United States, and spent long months every year visiting countries from Norway to Egypt. In 1880 and 1888, they left on year-long trips abroad. Yet he was frail in body and health, weighing less than 100 pounds and suffering from malaria. Obviously, his performance satisfied his neighbors, for they kept him in important jobs. Quite a guy—despite his physical appearance. He died at the age of ninety in 1919.

John C. Ostrom

John C. Ostrom lived in Brockport for probably eighteen years and left a lasting mark on the community. Carol Hannan did much of the research for this essay. I also had valuable help from Charlie Cowling.

Ostrom was born in 1797 in Schenectady, Dutchess County. He was of Dutch ancestry and his surname originally began with a double "o." He emigrated west and became a prosperous farmer in Ridgeway, Orleans County.

He was living in Ridgeway at the time of the 1840 U.S. census. However, he seems to have been living in Brockport by 1841 or 1842. His son, Walter B., was described by a Brockport Collegiate Institute student as having been a "village boy" before he enrolled in the B.C.I. in 1842. Another of John C.'s sons, John D., was also a student at the B.C.I. in 1842. John D. was also a student in 1844, 1845, 1846, and 1850 and Walter studied there in 1844, 1845, 1846, and 1850. Also, John C.'s daughter, Julia, was a B.C.I. student in 1844, 1845, 1846, and 1852—the last year as a music student. John C. and his family appear as residents of Sweden in the 1850 U.S. and

1855 N.Y.S. censuses. Walter joined the California Gold Rush after his graduation in 1850 and died of disease crossing Mexico.

Sometime after John C.'s arrival in Brockport, he invested in a commercial building on Main Street. The building burned in November 1860 and was described in the *Brockport Republic* at that time as "an old brick building, in a very poor condition, and of but little value." He also served as village clerk in 1856

In 1853, Ostrom bought the large lot on the corner of Main and South Streets and built a farm barn where the carriage house now stands. The rest of the lot was called "the Ostrom commons." James Cornes said in a *Brockport Democrat* article of reminiscences that the commons had a large boulder in the center and that the commons "were grown up with weeds, cattails and old Canal thistle. A foot path ran diagonally from northwest to south east through these commons and through this path most of the travel was done by people living in the south east part of the village." The village boys played soldier there, using the boulder as a fort and the cattails and bull thistles as the enemy. The boulder was 50 or 60 feet north of where the Morgan-Manning House is now located and, probably, is buried 8 or 10 feet down.

Tradition says that Ostrom built a small house on South Street where he lived until the Morgan-Manning House was finished. He probably began construction of the Morgan-Manning House in 1854. Its site at the corner of South and Main Streets was swampy, which may explain why South Street is not aligned with Monroe Avenue. It may have been designed to skirt the swampy area.

The need to drain the building lot may also explain why construction seems to have taken so long, for an item in the *Brockport Republic* of October 31, 1856, reports: "Among the many buildings now being constructed, there is none that will add more to the beauty of our village than the house of Mr. Ostrom. It will cost, when completed over $12,000."

Ostrom next appears in the *Brockport Republic* on March 1, 1860, with an account of "A very fine party ... at their magnificent residence ... on the occasion of the second anniversary of their daughter's ... marriage." The article reports that "gas has been introduced, and the light sent forth from the elegant chandeliers [sic] added new brilliancy to their hitherto spacious and resplendent parlors. One of these chandeliers cost $150." The *Republic* boasted that "The spaciousness and splendor of Mr. Ostrom's residence is now equaled by but two other residences in the county" and concluded that "As Mr. Ostrom is now rated the wealthiest man in the town, of course he 'can stand it.'"

The *Republic* did not comment on Ostrom's health on that festive occasion, but it could not have been very robust, for the *Republic* reported on May 10—two months later—that "the recovery of Mr. John Ostrom is considered very doubtful. His situation is deemed very critical." He died on May 19 of a "tumor on the neck", aged fifty-nine, and was buried in Medina.

Ostrom's widow inherited the house and sold it to Thomas P. Eldridge who was married to her daughter, Julia. They resided in Brooklyn, where Thomas was "a salesman for a dry goods jobbing house," which he later headed. They rented the house to roomers. In 1864, they sold the house to James Guild for $7,000. One of his tenants was Dayton S. Morgan. In 1867, Morgan bought the house for $9,000 and lived there until his death in 1890. Morgan's widow inherited the house. In 1896, the Morgans' daughter, Sarah Morgan Manning, whose husband had died in 1895, moved into the house. She bought it in 1934 for $10,000 and lived there until her death in the fire that badly damaged the house in 1964.

In her will, Sarah Morgan Manning left the house to some educational or cultural organization. The Western Monroe Historical Society was organized for the purpose of acquiring the property, which it did in 1967. With the fire damage repaired by members of the W.M.H.S., the house that John Ostrom built more than a century and a half ago remains a monument to him as a very valuable asset in the community where he resided for a relatively-short time.

Hiel Brockway

Hiel Brockway, co-founder of Brockport, was born in Old Lyme, Conn., in 1775. His forename came from the biblical hero who rebuilt Jericho after it had been destroyed by Joshua. His father had been a patriot hero during the Revolutionary War. In 1798, he married Phebe Merrill, a descendant of John and Priscilla Alden.

The young couple moved west, farming on the way, to Catskill, NY, then on to Seneca, then to Phelps, then again to Sweden. In 1820, he opened a brick tavern and, a bit later, a grist mill in Clarkson. He also founded a brickyard on Clinton Street in Brockport, using clay from, I believe, a field northeast of Clarkson Corners. Some of the brick walls in businesses on the west side of Main Street seem to have come from his brickyard.

Beginning in 1817, Brockway bought land in Sweden on the west side of Lake Road and on the east side north of what is now Water Street where the canal was expected to come, paying $4,399.39, or $5.46 an acre. Later, he bought land on the east side of Lake Road from members of James Seymour's financially troubled syndicate.

Although Brockway shares with Seymour the title of co-founder of Brockport, he played a much greater role in the life of the village than did his partner. Seymour moved to Rochester in 1826. Brockway spent the rest of his life in the village, where he was a leader in civic and commercial affairs. Brockway seems never to have engaged in political activities, though two of his sons-in-law became Brockport's only members of the U.S. Congress.

Brockway remained active in the real estate business, developing, selling, and building residential and commercial properties. He built a boatyard alongside his brickyard on Clinton Street and a dry dock west of them. He also built part of the canal in Brockport. In 1828, he opened the first packet line on the canal from Rochester to Buffalo. Later, he extended his Red Bird line to Albany. In 1832, he was also one of the unsuccessful petitioners for charters for a railroad and a bank.

A major Brockway legacy to the village resulted from his role in the effort to found an institution of higher education in the village. In 1830, he joined a group of Brockporters who invited the Baptist Missionary Convention of Western New York to locate in Brockport the college it planned. He offered the Baptists 6 acres of land and $3,000 as an inducement to select Brockport and it was accepted. Though the Baptist College did not become established, the building that the villagers provided became the progenitor of what is now the State University of New York College at Brockport.

Brockway died August 19, 1842, at the age of sixty-seven. His son-in-law, Elias B. Holmes, carried on his packet line for a few years, but the boatyard and brickyard burned in 1848 and the packet line expired in 1852 with the arrival of the railroad.

George R. Ward

George R. Ward was a most remarkable Brockporter but little remembered today. He was born in Pavilion in 1837 and came to Brockport about 1854. He began in the grocery business in 1860. In 1871, he bought the building at 72 Main Street and remodeled it to a height of three stories. The grocery was on the ground floor and, in 1878, he added an opera house on the third floor.

With the opera house as his base, he was Brockport's leading impresario. He hosted in the opera house concerts, operas, public lectures (including Elizabeth Cady Stanton), meetings, suppers, plays, parties, a dog circus, minstrel shows, a human serpent, a comedian, wrestling and boxing matches, dancing assemblies, and, for a time, a roller skating rink. He sponsored performances on a circuit to Albion, Medina, and Batavia.

Ward also organized many other recreational activities. He sponsored musical tournaments, baseball games, festivals, excursions and fat man, bicycle, and fire hose races. One festival included a procession through the village with twelve bands, twenty-three units, and the mayor of Rochester. One excursion by a special, twelve-car train from Rochester to Niagara Falls included over 300 Brockporters, plus hundreds from other towns. Another eleven-car special train took Rochester-area tourists to the 1876 American centennial celebration in Philadelphia.

In 1880 and 1881, he held "Grand Mid-Summer Tournaments" with a balloon flight; bicycle, fat man, and horse races; a tight-rope walker; and a target shoot. Special trains brought Rochesterians to the event, boosting the attendance to 6,000. He offered a $200 prize for the "handsomest woman in New York State." Unfortunately, the "handsomest woman" was regarded by many as not being especially attractive and was revealed a week later to have entered under a false name. She became insane and was confined to an asylum. In 1882, the summer event became a "Carnival of All Nations," with an attendance of 2,500. It included a 10-mile ladies horseback race that was to determine the "championship of the world."

Ward was involved in many civic activities, organizing the annual Decoration Day celebrations, firemen's parades, an "Old Folks" concert, and Fourth of July celebrations. He was a charter member and first foreman of a fire company and was mainly responsible for bringing the 1876 steamer to Brockport. He organized a program to host "fresh air" children from New York City. He chaired the committee to raise funds to erect the Soldiers and Sailors Monument. In 1887, he was assistant secretary of the State Fair and organized its Domestic Hall. In 1877, he was general superintendent of the Brockport Union Agricultural Fair. He was an active member of the Literary Society, the Reading Room Committee, and the Temperance Society.

Ward was a talented musician, performing publicly as a solo vocalist, in a men's quartet, or in a chorus many times. He was music director for the Presbyterian Church and the Brockport Opera Club and a band and choir conductor.

Ward was a leader in the local Republican organization, chairing it, serving as a delegate to district, Congressional District, and state nominating conventions and as president of the Young Men's Political Club (at the age of fifty). In 1872, he was vice-president of the Sweden Grant Club. He was a village trustee (1878–1880), board president six times (1881–1889), and was a member of the village's Board of Health. He ran unsuccessfully for county sheriff in 1872 and for county treasurer in 1876. He was also a supporter of the Prohibition Party.

In business—besides his grocery store (which he sold in 1887), the opera house, and his work as an impresario—he was one of the founders of the Moore-Shafer Shoe Mfg. Co., a trustee of the Rochester Fire Escape Co., manager of a telephone company, sold insurance, and owned a phosphate warehouse. He had a contract to service the village's kerosene street lights. In 1885, he went bankrupt, but somehow managed to retain ownership of his grocery and the opera house.

The *Brockport Republic* said of him: "When he takes hold of an enterprise ... it has to go, for he always enlists the co-operation of those whose assistances are requisite." He accomplished all of that and more despite being chronically ill throughout that period, often home-bound or hospitalized. He died February 14, 1889, aged fifty-one.

Who Left for Greener Pastures

The Reverend Benjamin Titus Roberts

The Reverend Benjamin Titus Roberts had been ordained as a Methodist Episcopal preacher in 1848, but began to become disaffected with some practices in that denomination by 1852 when he was a pastor in Buffalo. From 1853 to 1855, he was pastor in Brockport and began to preach his doctrines to a group of his followers in services at the former Free Will Baptist church on King Street. They became known as Nazarites.

In 1855, Roberts was transferred to Albion, but continued to hold services in Brockport. In December 1856, the Methodists' Quarterly Conference, meeting in Brockport, denounced the Nazarites for "seeking to disturb and divide the Church by publicly assailing the Christian character of her ministers and members" and alleged:

> ... their meetings have been characterized by vulgarisms; loud laughter, bitter censoriousness, horrid unnatural screaming; repeating the same words twenty or thirty times, throwing about their arms and limbs, both of men and women in a manner shocking, not only to religion but to common decency.

The Nazarites held a camp meeting in Clarkson at the same time.

From December 1856 until April 1857, the Nazarites and the mainstream Methodists battled it out in the columns of the *Brockport Republic*, publishing thirteen long letters denouncing one another. The conflict continued within the Methodist Episcopal denomination until, while serving in Pekin, New York, in 1860, Roberts broke away and organized the Free Methodist denomination. It was "Free" because it discontinued the Methodist practice of charging for the use of its pews and because it took an abolitionist position on slavery. Also, Roberts edited a journal, the *Earnest Christian*, wrote several books, and founded the Cheesbrough Seminary in North Chili, now Roberts Wesleyan College. He died in 1893.

Two of Roberts's successors in the Brockport pulpit and at least three of his Brockport converts became early Free Methodist clergymen and another published his pamphlets. A Free Methodist church was founded in Brockport in 1875 and is now located on Fourth Section Road. The denomination now has 77,000 members in the United States with 107,000 average attendance at Sunday services and 850,000 members worldwide.

William H. Cooley

William H. Cooley was a fifth-generation Brockporter born here in 1852. His father, Levi, Jr., was the architect for the original building for the Brockport Normal School. William graduated from the Brockport State Normal School and began studies at the University of Rochester when his father died requiring that he return to Brockport to close out his father's business, then he studied law but never took the bar exam. Nevertheless, he practiced as a patent attorney in Rochester. He invented mechanical and electrical appliances and held forty or fifty patents on them.

Walter J. Kingsley

Walter J. Kingsley was born in Holley in 1874, but he was living in Brockport by 1880 and attended the Brockport Normal School in 1890. He began a highly successful career as a journalist and press agent working for his brother's newspaper in Buffalo. He had a very varied career as reporter, managing editor, foreign correspondent, theater manager, POW in Manchuria, amateur boxer and bicycle racer, apprentice seaman, talent scout, publicist, and spy.

Early in his career, he was a foreign correspondent for the London *Daily Mail* and other British papers in China, Korea, and Japan. He covered the Boer War in South Africa and the Russo-Japanese War of 1904. In the latter conflict, he was alleged to have been a spy for the Japanese government.

He was best known, however, as "one of the highest paid press agents" for vaudeville, Broadway theaters, book publishers, and so on. Among many other celebrity clients, he represented the Ziegfield Follies. One newspaper said that "the amount of press stuff he gets into the newspapers is something appalling. He has the hypnotic eye, surely."

He was much given to pulling publicity stunts. For instance, he made claims of huge wagers on the America's Cup to draw attention to the underdog crew and wrote letters to ethics boards about the scandalous nature of books and plays to boost their sales. He was the first writer to use the word "jazz" to refer to the music genre, but he did so in a fraudulent claim to have learned of its origins. One etymologist referred to him as "the glib master of baloney and hoopla." Kingsley was the first person for whom Broadway dimmed its lights as a memorial.

Kingsley was married twice, first to silent film actress Alma Hanlon. They had a daughter, Dorothy, who became a successful Hollywood scriptwriter. Among her credits were the *Bob Hope Show*, the *Edgar Bergen Hour*, films starring Esther Williams, Jane Powell, and Debbie Reynolds, *Seven Brides for Seven Brothers*, and *Angels in the Outfield*. She died in 1996 at the age of eighty-seven. After the divorce from Hanlon, he married Francesca Carmen, a Hungarian-born dancer.

He died of cerebral spinal meningitis in 1929 after being found unconscious outside the New Amsterdam Theater. He was cremated and his wife cast his ashes from a plane flying over Broadway. His estate had only $3,000, probably because he gave so much away. A colleague wrote in *The New York Times*:

> No one will ever know the extent of his helpfulness. Much has been said about the hundreds of girls he assisted. A list of the men he helped would be just as long. A suit of clothes for a road agent down on his luck …; a night's lodging here, a board bill there; five and ten dollar bills by the hundreds to the fellows who needed a "stake." … The overcoats he bought would stock a store. Many's the man who enjoyed a comfortable … summer … in the country at Kingsley's expense. There were doctors' bills, hospital bills and railroad tickets back home without number.

Twice his colleagues elected him president of the Theatrical Press Representatives of America. A biographer says: "He was well loved by the theatrical community and there were many op-eds and memorials written of him after his death." Another was extravagant and even rhapsodic in praising him. Among other things, he described his virtues as generous, fearless, hardworking, cheerful, humorous, playful, adventurous, and patient. He said: "Kingsley was a man everybody knew—rich man, poor man, beggar man, thief—and everybody liked." He was "one of the greatest of the 'star-makers' and 'trail-blazers.'"

Charles B. Greenough

Charles B. Greenough was born in Fairhaven, Vt., in 1834 and came to Brockport with his family as a boy. He was first employed as the agent of a canal transportation company. Later, he became the general ticket agent of the Erie Railroad and, in 1863, general passenger agent of the New York Central Railroad in New York City. Still later, he became chief engineer and general manager of the Bleecker Street & Fulton Ferry Rail Road in New York.

Greenough had a disagreement with his New York company and wanted to build a railway of his own. He heard of developments in Brazil, traveled to Rio de Janeiro, bought Mauá's concession in November 1866, and founded the Botanical Garden Rail Road Company. The Brazilian government was reluctant to allow another foreigner to build another street railway in its capital, but permission was finally granted on June 22, 1868, in the midst of Brazil's war with Paraguay. Emperor Dom Pedro II presided at the inauguration of Rio de Janeiro's second tramway, Greenough's 3-km line from the Rua do Ouvidor to the Largo do Machado, on October 9, 1868.

Greenough had tramway experience, seventeen stockholders, and $500,000, and his line was a great success. Within six weeks, the route was extended to Botafogo, and by July 1869, there were nineteen streetcars running in Rio de Janeiro, all built by John Stephenson in New York. The first cars were closed models, but open trams appeared in 1870 and established the design for all the tram companies in Rio de Janeiro and most other cities in Brazil. On January 1, 1871, the line reached the Botanical Garden, 10 km from downtown. By 1879, the company had telephone communication between its tram stations. Because it was elaborately built, well managed, and served the affluent neighborhoods on the south side of Rio de Janeiro, the Botanical Garden Rail Road became the prestige tramway system in Brazil. The track gauge was the same as the streetcar lines in New York. Greenough died in 1880.

Carl Ethan Akeley

Carl Ethan Akeley lived in Brockport for only a short time in his youth. However, that experience had an important effect on his life and career. He was born in Clarendon in 1864 and attended school for only three years.

Akeley had an older brother, Lewis, who recalled when he was ninety-nine years old that, as boys, he and Carl worked on the farm: "While plowing I carried my Greek grammer [*sic.*] with me and memorized it. Carl on the other hand had eyes only for the natural life around him." Lewis pursued an academic career, eventually serving as Dean of Engineering at the University of South Dakota. One of his students received the Nobel Prize in Physics for inventing the cyclotron and credited Akeley for inspiring him to become a scientist. He began at U.S.D. in 1887 and was still there seventy-four years later when he died at the age of 100.

Carl came to Brockport as a teenager and enrolled at the State Normal School, but soon dropped out and was employed by David Bruce. As a child, he had developed an avid fascination with a crude form of taxidermy and studied that art with Bruce. After that short apprenticeship with Bruce, he pursued a career in that field and became "the father of modern taxidermy."

In 1883, at Bruce's urging, nineteen-year-old Akeley went to work as a taxidermy apprentice at Ward's Natural Science Establishment in Rochester. While there, he mounted the hide of P. T. Barnum's elephant, Jumbo, the largest remains of an animal ever, until that time, to be subjected to a taxidermist's efforts. After leaving Ward's, he pursued his career at the Milwaukee Public Museum (1886–92), as a private contractor (1892–96), at the Field Museum of Natural History (1896–1909), and the American Museum of Natural History (1909–26).

Along the way, he refined taxidermy techniques. Before Akeley, taxidermy consisted of stuffing animal hides with straw or some similar material, with little regard to the actual shape of the live bodies. He fitted the animal skins over carefully prepared and sculpted hollow manikins in the form of the animals' bodies, producing very lifelike specimens, with consideration of musculature, wrinkles, and veins.

Akeley also created the modern museum diorama. He placed mounted specimens in recreations of their natural habitat with painted scenes appropriate to the locale in the background. He created the Akeley Hall of African Mammals at the American Museum of Natural History. He began work on it in 1909, collecting specimens, planning, painting scenes, etc. The center of the hall is occupied by a herd of eight elephants. Recessed into the surrounding wall are twenty-eight dioramas of other African mammals, all presented in their natural environments. It is still the greatest museum diorama in the world despite being nearly a century old. Akeley died before the African Hall was completed in 1926. One of the dioramas features a mountain gorilla. Akeley had sketched the landscape to use for its backdrop.

Additionally, Akeley had conducted the first scientific study of the mountain gorillas and had persuaded King Leopold of Belgium to create the Virunga National Park, the first national park in Africa, to protect them. He died of a tropical disease and was buried at the spot depicted in the gorilla diorama. Searchers later located his grave by referring to that sketch.

Akeley was also an explorer (especially in Somaliland and British East Africa), inventor, the holder of more than thirty patents, and author of several books. One of his inventions was a "cement gun" called shotcrete. Another was a motorized movie camera capable of following a moving animal, which Akeley used to capture more accurately the shapes of animals in motion. He escorted Theodore Roosevelt on one of his expeditions and George Eastman on another.

The World Taxidermy & Fish Carving Championships awards gold medallions that bear Carl Akeley's likeness to its "Best in the World" honorees. The taxidermy profession regards Akeley as its patron saint. When the Clarendon Historical Society held a ceremony to commemorate the sesquicentennial of Akeley's birth in 2014, the president and the executive secretary of the American Taxidermy Association traveled to Clarendon for the event.

Richard Cutts Shannon

Richard Cutts Shannon came to Brockport in 1903, aged sixty-four, after a career as a soldier, diplomat, lawyer, and politician. For the next seventeen years, he was one of Brockport's more distinguished residents until his death in 1920, aged eighty-one.

Shannon was born in New London, Conn., in 1839, attended schools in Biddeford, Me., and graduated from Waterville (now Colby) College. When that college closed at the outset of the Civil War, Shannon enlisted in the Union Army and was soon commissioned a first lieutenant. He served as *aide-de-camp* to a general, and in October 1862, he was a captain and assistant adjutant general. He was taken prisoner at Chancellorsville in May 1863 and spent eighteen days in Libby Prison. After the war, he was promoted to brevet lieutenant colonel.

In 1871, he was appointed secretary of the U.S. legation in Rio de Janeiro, Brazil, where he was *chargé d'affaires* twice. He resigned in 1875 to take charge of the Botanical Gardens Railroad Co. His associate in that venture was Charles Backus Greenough of Brockport, who was married to the former Martha Ann Spaulding of Clarkson.

He returned to the U.S. in 1883 and graduated from the Columbia College law school in 1885, passed the bar in 1886, and entered the practice of law. Greenough had died in 1880 and Shannon married his widow in 1887. From 1891 to 1893, he was U.S. Minister to Nicaragua, El Salvador, and Costa Rico. He was elected as a Republican to Congress in 1894 and re-elected twice, but did not run for a fourth term and resumed the practice of law. In 1903, he retired and they moved to Brockport.

He bought the large house on the northwest corner of Main and College Streets that had been built for Dr. Thacher by Luther Gordon and undertook extensive remodeling. He and his wife were generous benefactors of the village. Shannon Hall in the Baptist Church is named for them. His wife paid $250,000 to save a relative's bank from insolvency. He was also a loyal *alumnus* of Colby College, funding the Shannon Physical Laboratory building and an astronomical observatory. He received an honorary degree from Colby in 1892. Shannon died in 1920.

H. Miles Moore

H. Miles Moore was born in Brockport in 1826. Both of his parents died before his first birthday and he was reared by his grandfather. He graduated from Brockport public schools and Union College, studied law with Henry R. Selden and Simeon Jewett and passed the bar in 1848. He moved to Louisiana where he practiced law and ran a plantation. In 1850, he moved to Missouri, practiced law, and edited a newspaper. In 1854, he moved across the river and helped found Leavenworth, Kansas, the heart of the free-state effort. He proposed its name, was its first secretary, and drew up its incorporation papers. Though he had been a slave owner in Louisiana, he became an ardent abolitionist in Kansas.

Moore was a general in the Free-State Army, a delegate to the 1855 free-state Topeka Constitutional Convention, attorney general for three terms, U.S. commissioner, and assistant U.S. attorney. He served in both the territorial and the state legislatures and as a cavalry colonel in the Union Army. After the war, he served in the state legislature, as Leavenworth City Attorney for three terms, as city court judge, and on the school board for many years.

Moore was a leader in the effort that resulted in "Bloody Kansas" becoming a free state through a struggle that was, in effect, a dress rehearsal for the American Civil War. He died in 1909 from a runaway horse accident.

Richard Joseph Welch

Richard Joseph Welch was born on Lyman Street in Brockport in 1869, but pursued a distinguished career in California and is known as the "Father of the Golden Gate Bridge." He moved to San Francisco with his family at the age of fifteen, but visited his hometown frequently and retained ownership of the house in which he had been born for many years and later tried to buy it back.

In California, he first worked on a farm and then as an iron molder and machinist. He entered politics in 1896 by campaigning for presidential candidate William McKinley and organized San Francisco's Dewey Republican Club in 1898. In 1900, he was appointed clerk of the San Francisco County Superior Court. He then served in the State Senate (1901–13) and on the San Francisco Board of Supervisors (1916–26). Meanwhile, he was San Francisco's harbormaster (1903–07).

While on the board of supervisors, Welch introduced the legislation to build the Golden Gate Bridge. He had been the harbormaster at the time of the 1906 earthquake and believed that the city needed another escape route in time of disaster. He served on the board of directors of its governing authority from its formation in 1928 until his death. He also promoted construction of the Bay Bridge.

In 1926, Welch was elected to the U.S. House of Representatives from a San Francisco district to fill a vacancy caused by the death of the incumbent. He was re-elected repeatedly, usually without opposition, until he died in office in 1949 at the age of eighty, *en route* to a Congressional committee meeting, having served in Congress for twenty-three years and in public service for forty-nine years.

In Congress, he called himself a Progressive Republican and sponsored and supported legislation that benefited labor, farmers, small businesses, San Francisco, and California. Two future speakers of the House of Representatives, Joseph Martin and Sam Rayburn, were among the many Congressmen who eulogized him in a memorial service in the nation's capital. California's Governor Earl Warren said that "he had contributed greatly to the development of our state."

John Hall Deane

John Hall Deane was born in Canada in 1842 and moved with his family to Rochester when very young. By the time he enrolled at the Brockport Collegiate Institute at the age of seventeen, he was an orphan with a Rochester residence. He attended the school for four years, paying "his way ... by ringing the bell and sawing a cord of hard wood ... each week day."

Deane seems to have been a very good student. At the closing exercises in 1860, he delivered a "Declamation" entitled "Creation". In 1861, the subject of his oration was "God in American History." In 1862, his address, "March of Time," was the only presentation commented upon in the *Brockport Republic*, which said that it "was very emphatically applauded." Three months later, the *Republic* reported that his oration "will be published next week. It was received at his delivery with marks of great approval."

After completing his studies at the B.C.I., Deane enrolled at the University of Rochester, but soon dropped out to enlist in the Union Army. He spoke at a war meeting held to facilitate enlistments in Captain Milo Starks's Company "A" of the 140th N.Y.V.I. His address was called "Eloquent and patriotic" by the *Republic.* He then enlisted in Company "A" as fifth sergeant.

On the second day at Gettysburg, according to a letter he wrote to his sister that was published in the *Republic*, he obtained permission from Captain Starks to "leave the company a few minutes." He went to a nearby house in search of "something to eat for the boys in the company." When he left the house, "an officer rode up and demanded what [he] was doing there." Instead of accepting Deane's explanation, the officer took him to a "Brigade Provost Marshal's Headquarters." When he was released after several hours, he was unable to find his regiment.

He joined a unit of "Pennsylvania Reserves" and fought in the Battle at Cemetery Hill. He was wounded there in the leg and taken to a field hospital. A Louisiana regiment captured the hospital and took its inmates as prisoners. Deane was sent to Libby Prison in Richmond, but was quickly exchanged and sent to Annapolis. There a young man offered to take him on a tour of the city, but instead drugged him and delivered him to the U.S. Navy, which conscripted him as a seaman on the mortar schooner *John Smith*. So he was discharged in September 1865 from the U.S. Navy.

After the war, he earned a B.A. in 1866 and an M.A. in 1870 from the University of Rochester. He then became a lawyer in New York City and speculated in real estate. He claimed to have accumulated a fortune of $3 million, the equivalent of $360 million today. He was said to have built 600 houses in New York City and to have been "one of the oldest and most intimate friends of John D. Rockefeller." He and Rockefeller were said to have founded one of the Baptist churches in New York City.

He was a very generous benefactor. In response to a plea from the pulpit for fundraising, he placed a donation of $100,000 in the collection plate of the Calvary Baptist Church in N.Y.C. He donated $110,000 to the University of Rochester including endowments for four scholarships for graduates of the B.C.I. He paid $4,000 for an organ for Brockport's First Baptist Church. He made donations to Vassar College, $15,000 to the Second Baptist Church of Harlem, $50,000 for a fund for the assistance of the sons of Baptist ministers, $50,000 to the building fund of the Calvary Baptist Church, and $38,000 to the American Baptist Home Missionary Society. He also presented "valuable books" to Horatio N. Beach's Free Library.

Deane was also quite active as a layman in Baptist organizations. He was president of the Baptist Sunday school Teachers' Association of N.Y.C. and vice-president of the N.Y.S. Baptist Convention. He delivered an address to the regular monthly meeting of the Baptist Social Union of Manhattan. However, when he suffered a severe financial reverse, the Calvary Baptist Church in an "unjust and therefore discreditable" action excommunicated him from the church and the denomination.

That financial failure occurred in 1884. Apparently, it resulted from an economic downturn that affected the value of his real estate investments. Estimates of the amount of the claims against him ranged from $538,602.15 to $1 million, but he was also reported to have assets of greater value than his debts. In any case, by 1890, the *Republic* said that he had "worked his way out, met all his obligations, and [was] again realizing prosperity." Nevertheless, in 1909, he said that he had not settled all of the 1884 claims against him and owned only his "clothes and $7."

Deane was also a published author. *The National Tribune* published a long article by him, "Torpedo Boats of the Rebellion," in 1901, including some of his experiences. One of those boats is depicted in the illustrations section of this book.

Through all of this, Deane maintained an active interest in Brockport and was a loyal *alumnus* of the B.C.I. He continued to subscribe to the *Republic* and it published a long letter from him recounting some of his experiences at the B.C.I. He explained his desire to read the *Republic*: "I once knew 400 boys and girls in that vicinity and went to school with them and have kept track of many of them. I love to see their names in the old paper once in a while." He was elected second vice-president of the New York Association of Brockporters and *Alumni* in 1904. He entertained a Brockporter in N.Y.C. and visited the village several times. He died in June 1923.

Who Contributed at Home and Abroad

Davis Carpenter

Davis Carpenter was born in Walpole, N.H., in 1799, with nine siblings and five half-siblings from his father's earlier marriage. He studied medicine in Middlebury College in Vermont, graduating in 1824. He then studied law and passed the bar, but he seems never to have practiced. He arrived in Brockport in 1825 and became Brockport's second physician and was, also, the senior partner in a store that sold books and drugs.

He married Azubah (1810–81), one of Hiel Brockway's daughters, in 1825. He was active in local civic affairs. In 1831, he was the village treasurer. He also served as health officer and colonel in the militia. He was active in the firefighting companies, being chief engineer of the No. 2 company in 1838; he also served as a fire chief for several years.

He was a perennial leader of the local Republican Party. He was often selected as a convention delegate and a leading speaker at meetings and rallies. In the Lincoln campaign of 1860, he chaired rallies and commanded the "Wide Awakes," the para-military Republican youth organization. He attended Lincoln's inauguration. In 1867, he chaired an enormous Republican campaign meeting for the twenty-eighth Congressional District that was attended by a crowd estimated at 7,000.

During the Civil War, he often chaired war meetings. In one of his speeches, he said the "institution [of slavery] must be extirpated if we would be successful." He was one of the more successful recruiters for the Union Army.

Carpenter was elected to Congress in 1853 to fill a vacancy and served until 1855. He was defeated for re-election, but unsuccessfully sought the Republican nomination for Congress again in 1862.

Carpenter owned a farm in Hamlin and was a prize-winning horse breeder.

After his defeat, he returned to the practice of medicine. He suffered ill health beginning in 1874 at the age of seventy-five and died in 1878. He is buried in the High Street cemetery.

Fred W. Hill

Fred W. Hill was one of four Monroe County District School commissioners (later superintendents) for some thirty-seven years. His district included the towns of Clarkson, Greece, Hamlin, Parma, and Sweden. He was first elected in 1902 and was still in office in late 1939. (I have been unable to learn when he actually retired.)

Hill graduated from Fairport High School and from Yale University. He began a career as a school teacher in district schools in the Town of Sweden and Adams Basin. He then served as principal of the Spencerport High School for seven years before being elected district commissioner against seven opponents on the seventh ballot. After that, he was repeatedly re-elected without opposition. His leadership in that position was recognized state-wide when he was elected president of the State District Superintendents Assn.

Hill was very much a hands-on administrator. He made frequent visits to the schools in his district, held many meetings for teachers and school administrators, conducted literacy tests for new voters, and ran college scholarship competitions. He served on official health committees and organized educational exhibits for State Fairs. He was a "Guarantor" of Brockport's Chautauqua and the main instigator of the Monroe County Traveling Library. A photo of him with that library appears in the illustration section of this book. It was mainly through his efforts that the Brockport Central School District was created.

He owned a farm in Adams Basin and, in 1925, bought the Root farm in the Town of Sweden. In 1925, he bought the house at 299 Main Street from the well-known artist Bertha Coleman and moved from Adams Basin to Brockport.

The Fred W. Hill Elementary School bears his name.

David Bruce

David Bruce, scientist, painter, naturalist, and taxidermist, was born in Perth, Scotland, on June 30, 1833, and moved with his family to Norwich, England, when he was less than a year old. He early developed an interest in birds, butterflies, and painting. At the age of eighteen, he met the great English entomologist William C. Hewitson, who recognized his talent and encouraged him to devote his life to scientific illustration.

Later that year, he traveled to New Zealand following a girlfriend. He soon tired of her and set off for Australia and then returned to England. He married in England, but his wife, named Fisher, died and he remarried Rachel Marshall, also in England, but was in Paris during the siege of 1871. About 1880, he emigrated to the U.S., settling in Brockport. What he did in the meantime is a bit of a mystery. He simply said in a letter in 1883: "I have since [after he was "less than a year old"] been knocking about in different parts of the world for 49 years."

In Brockport, he developed a career, painting murals in churches, hotels, and homes. He also became a painter of great skill using this talent in several ways. He would decorate the interior of homes in the Brockport area by tinting the hard-finished walls and painting tropical foliage and the bright hued birds found there. He also reproduced cattails in his paintings with authentic forms and colors. The sidewalls, staircases, and halls of these residences often displayed his work. He also did straight interior house painting; several of his murals in area homes have survived.

He was sufficiently successful in Brockport that, beginning in 1883, he could afford to take annual trips to the Colorado mountains to study birds, butterflies, and moths. His first trip to Colorado lasted only eight days, but he returned with 200 bird skins and several hundred butterflies and moths. Given his height (5 feet 7½ inches) and weight (200 lb.), he could not have been that agile chasing butterflies. His trip was abbreviated because he had been hired to do the interior of St. Luke's Episcopal Church.

Later, he was back in Colorado and returned to Colorado every year but three until 1897. As a result, according to F. Martin Brown, a fellow lepidopterist, "we know more about high altitude butterflies of Colorado than of any other high country in the world." Brown also said: "... his material now is found in the principal museums of the world."

In 1892, Bruce provided a collection of Colorado's moths and butterflies for the state's exhibit at the Chicago World Fair. In 1893, he sold his private collection to the University of Wisconsin, adding many specimens later until the university called a halt because it lacked the space. In 1931, the collection was transferred to the National Museum of Natural History in Washington. He also supplied specimens of butterflies and moths to the National Museum of Natural History. For instance, in 1889, the museum recorded "A series of 5 species of Lepidoptera from David Bruce ... all desiderata."

In 1894, he established for the first time that there were naturally hybrid butterflies and moths, saying: "Whoring is a recognized institution in all mining districts and the insects have taken to it as well as the genus Homo." Besides his work in Colorado, Bruce made extensive collections of birds, butterflies, and moths in Monroe and Orleans Counties.

Bruce was also a creative taxidermist. He was the first taxidermist to place birds and mammals in cases surrounded by their natural environment. His skill as a painter enabled him to reproduce suitable backgrounds for the mounted specimens.

Early in the twentieth century, about fifty cases of mounted birds and animals by David Bruce were displayed on an upper floor of the Powers Building in Rochester. The owner of the building exhibited them to attract people to his building. Carl Akeley, a farm boy from Clarendon, saw that exhibit at the age of twelve and was inspired by it to pursue taxidermy himself. Eventually, he studied taxidermy with Bruce and went on to found modern taxidermy. A little later, Bruce made a similar collection for what was then called the Mechanics Institute, now RIT.

Bruce never faked any of his work; he knew firsthand what he was reproducing. Brockporter Gifford Morgan had a very fine case of game birds in his study mounted by Bruce. They included male and female specimens of about a dozen native game birds. Bruce was mentioned several times in E. H. Eaton's two-volume study *Birds of New York*. Bruce had a retiring nature, but was exceptionally gifted, very accurate, and fast in the preparation of his work. His gift as an artist assisted him greatly in preparing the natural effect desired.

Bruce died on October 1, 1903, aged seventy. In its obituary, the *Brockport Republic* called him "quite a lecturer on taxidermy and the natural sciences."

George F. Guelph

George F. Guelph was born in Brockport in 1870 and left school at the age of twelve to begin a sixty-year career as a printer for the *Brockport Republic.* About the same time, he became interested in taxidermy and collected and processed birds' skins and animal pelts. He and David Bruce exchanged many specimens.

Guelph also worked on the Mechanics Institute (now RIT) collection and was a curator at Ward's Museum of Natural Science in Rochester. Ward's sent him to the 1893 Columbian Exposition in charge of one their exhibits. Nathan Davis, a Town of Sweden young man, learned taxidermy from Guelph. Later, he settled in the State of Washington. There he ran a store in connection with taxidermy and had an extensive fur business.

Guelph was an avid naturalist, hunting and camping in pursuit of that interest. He presented learned papers at natural science conferences. Guelph was a charter member, first "Fleet Captain," and second commodore of the Brockport Yacht Club, described by David Hale in his history of the B.Y.C. as "a major factor in the establishment of the Club and its racing program." Guelph was also commodore in 1912–13 and 1936–42. His ten-year service was the longest of any commodore in the history of the club. He built his own sailboat with which he won many races.

Guelph was also active in Brockport civic affairs, serving as an assistant fire chief for twenty years and claiming to have participated in sixty-three firemen's parades. He served as building inspector for the village and cemetery trustee. He was also a mechanic and photographer for the *Republic-Democrat.* This essay was, in part, adapted from the *Brockport Republic-Democrat*, November 25, 1954.

John Howe Kent

John Howe Kent began his career in Brockport and became the pre-eminent portrait photographer in America and a founder of the Eastman Kodak Co. Some of my information was provided by Carol Hannan from her research on historic Brockport houses.

Kent was born in Plattsburg, N.Y., in 1827, and moved to Brockport in 1848 to teach oil painting in the Brockport Collegiate Institute. He also practiced landscape painting. Charlotte Martin, in her 1929 Brockport history, says that he was "an artist of considerable ability in the painting of landscapes."

He and his family first rented an apartment at 45 State Street. Later, he lived at 89 Main Street, which we believe was the site of the Collins house. He sold that house in 1863 and moved to 55 Main Street. He married Julia Ainsworth in 1865 and moved again to the site where the Methodist Church is now. Soon after arriving in Brockport, he became interested in photography and opened Brockport's first photography studio, specializing in portraits. He continued to be listed in village directories as a "painter."

During his years in Brockport, he was active in the Republican Party. In particular, he was secretary for the Lincoln and Hamlin Wide Awakes, the paramilitary youth organization of the Republicans, in 1860. Kent also served on the committee that organized the Fourth of July celebration in 1857. He entered many examples of his work in the Brockport Agricultural Fair competition and won many first places, for landscape painting, marbling, ornamental writing, sign painting, card writing, oak graining, etc.

In 1868, after twenty years in Brockport, the house that his studio occupied was sold and he moved to Rochester. E. H. Jordan succeeded Kent and advertised that "Copies of Pictures from Kent's Negatives can be furnished on order."

Kent opened a studio at 58 State Street, Rochester. A biographer said that he quickly became "the leading photographer in Rochester and Western New York [and] enjoys a reputation which extends throughout the country." His studio was called "one of the most successful and prolific ... in the United States." Another biographer says that Kent did "more than any other artist in that line to establish the artistic character of the photograph." Still another says that "he had a clean style people today still find very classy. He didn't crowd his pictures, instead choosing to solely focus on the face of the sitter." Among those who posed for him were Horace Greeley, Susan B. Anthony, and Frederick Douglass.

At the Centennial Exposition in Philadelphia in 1876, Kent exhibited "the best and largest photographs ever made at that time ... receiving all the first prizes, five in number." He had a collection of 130,000 negatives. Other professional photographers regarded him highly enough to elect him president of the Photographers' Association of America in 1883. The George Eastman House has Kent photos in its permanent collection.

George Eastman frequented Kent's studio and called him one of the four men who taught him photography. George Selden of Clarkson was another visitor. Kent became one of the original stockholders and vice president of the Eastman Dry Plate & Film Co., with 100 shares as the fourth largest stockholder. Henry Strong was president and Eastman treasurer.

According to one biographer, Kent "tended to highly romanticize his subjects [and] manipulated lighting ... using his own hand-held screen creation that led to the collapsible hand-held reflectors many photographers still use today."

Kent's advice in the *British Journal of Photography* indicates the kind of portrait photographer he was:

> When your sitter is in the chair do not manipulate him and twist him this way and that way until you make him nervous; some people will stand it, but

> many will not. Engage him in conversation, converse with him on something that will interest him, get him in the best possible mood, and at the same time watch the light and the position of the head that will give the finest lines. A person cannot stand here, and have a good line here and another one there. Expose when the expression is right and most pleasant. Catch it in the shortest possible time and you will have a pleasant picture. I would rather give a man a good, pleasant picture than a first-class, exact picture, because it pleases him better.

Kent died in 1910, aged eighty-two. He had two children, but only a daughter, Ada Howe Kent, survived; she was an artist, never married, and left her fortune to the Ada Howe Kent Foundation. It had assets of $13 million in 2012 and made charitable donations of $460,500 for education and religious activities.

Asa Rowe

Asa Rowe built the finest rural house in the Town of Sweden, on Reed Road just west of Lake Road, using bricks that came to Brockport on the Erie Canal. His father, Abel, had arrived in the Town of Greece in 1805 and bought land on both sides of Ridge Road. He erected a "public house" on the site, one of only two frame dwellings between the Genesee and Niagara Rivers. He was supervisor of the Town of Greece twice.

Asa was born in Greece a year after his parents settled there. By 1824, he operated a hotel and a farm and had the first nursery and greenhouse in the county. He followed his father as Greece Town supervisor in 1834, 1835, and 1842. In 1828, he had married Ruby E. Reed, the daughter of a leading farmer in the Town of Sweden. In 1842–43, they moved to Sweden. In 1850, he was Supervisor of the Town of Sweden.

In 1853, he built the large Italianate mansion on 343 acres on Reed Road. He also owned a farm in Bergen. Merwin Austin was the architect for the house. Austin was a leading architect in western New York. Among his other projects was the second Monroe County Courthouse and the Brewster-Burke house in Rochester that was the longtime seat of the Landmark Society.

The architectural plans for the house and other material related to it were donated to the Town of Sweden Farmers' Museum by former owners Wesley Brown and his wife. They include a highly detailed contract between carpenter George Wilson and Rowe that includes specifics about the "privys" and a requirement that Rowe build Wilson a house on the property where he can live during the construction and provide a pasture for his cow. Wilson was to receive $1,000 for his work, which was begun in December 1852 and was to be completed by November 1853.

Rowe died in 1894. He was survived by three sons. One of them, George Henry, served in the Union Army and married another Ruby Reed. They had four children, one of whom, William, was a leading Brockport coal merchant. His son, George, was a longtime Brockport resident and George's son, another William, a great-great grandson of Asa, is a Clarkson resident.

Frederick P. Root

Frederick P. Root was, for many years, the largest landowner and farmer in the Town of Sweden and was also important in statewide agricultural circles. He had been born in Saratoga County in 1814 and came to Sweden by covered wagon with his family at the age of four.

His father died when Frederick was nineteen years old and, as the eldest son, Frederick became responsible for his family. Although he had little schooling, by avid reading, research, and study, he became well educated. He was a very active leader in promoting the interests of agriculture, sharing his knowledge by presenting lectures and learned papers to farm associations throughout the state. He was an organizer and first president of the N.Y.S. Farmers' Alliance.

He was also active in civic affairs, being elected to the N.Y.S. Assembly twice and serving as town supervisor, 1854–58. For many years, he was president of the Brockport Union Agricultural Society that ran the county fair and the Farmers' Co-operative Insurance Co.

Root Road is named for him. He outlived two wives and two of his three children and died in November 1904 at the age of ninety.

3

Notable Brockport Women

Mary Jane Holmes

Mary Jane Holmes is well known to Brockporters as the prolific and popular novelist. They may not know such details as that she wrote novels under some forty-seven titles, published some seventeen short stories, twenty-seven of her novels were first published as serials in magazines, or that her novels sold an estimated 3 million copies—many in pirated editions. Her readership was much broader than that indicates, because, she said, some at least of her work was syndicated to "forty or fifty" newspapers.

Holmes is also noteworthy for much that was not connected to her fame as a novelist. She and her husband, Daniel, were avid travelers. Based on that travel, she wrote at least eleven travel articles for the *Brockport Republic*, the *Brockport Democrat*, the Rochester *Democrat & Chronicle*, and the *Ladies Home Journal*. A newspaper in Tacoma, Wash., said that it published "frequent" articles by her. She also gave many, many talks based on her travels, including on Alaska, Rome, Scandinavia, Russia, Egypt, Venice, the Eastern countries, and Italy. *Ladies Home Journal* published her article on the Oberammergau festival. She also lectured in the greater Rochester area on many other topics—the Lake poets, Brockport history, Bunker Hill, American art and literature, hospitality, Easter, the Pilgrims, etc. She wrote an article for the *Ladies Home Journal* on "Good Husbands."

Holmes was an active leader in the Brockport community. She was a devout member of St. Luke's Episcopal Church, tithed to it, led the St. Luke's Guild, and taught Sunday school classes for many years. She was the perennial president of the

Women's Union Charitable Society that raised money for Brockport's poor, a regent of the D.A.R., and a member of the History Club and the Whist Club.

The Holmeses entertained frequently. Although they had no children of their own, Holmes went out of her way to befriend and entertain the children in the community, including students in the Normal School. They frequently threw elaborate parties that were the community's social events of the year. They had as many as "200–300" guests with two bands providing music and elaborate decorations. Her obituary in the *Brockport Republic* described her as the "leading spirit in all the social life" of the village.

Perhaps Holmes's most lasting legacy was her contributions to the struggle for equal rights for women. She was a leader in a countywide Women's Rights Association. More important was the influence of her writing. Unique among the women novelists of her day, Holmes wrote of ordinary people in everyday situations in a style that was infused with irony and humor and was accessible to the barely literate women and teenage girls of that time. She used that access to give her readers "a picture of a modern woman who rises in the world much as a man does, by self-betterment and looking to the main chance." Given her large audience and her subtle message, I believe that Holmes did more than any other writer of her time to condition American women to accept the leadership of the women's rights movements of the late nineteenth and early twentieth centuries.

Fannie Barrier Williams

Fannie Barrier Williams was well known as a civil rights leader in the Midwest, but other aspects of the Barrier family's place in her home community and the range of her reformist activities may be less well known.

Fannie's father, Anthony, was born in Philadelphia in 1824 and came to Brockport in 1829 (presumably with his family). In 1849, he married Harriet Prince. He became a barber at a young age and pursued that occupation until his death at the age of sixty-five in 1890, being identified as "the principal barber in our village." He also was a coal dealer for a few years.

The Barriers were leading members of the First Baptist Church. He was a trustee, a clerk, its treasurer for ten years, and a deacon his last six years. They both taught Sunday school classes for many years and Harriet was active in the Women's Baptist Foreign Mission Society and was an officer in the Women's Christian Temperance Union.

The Barriers were good friends of Frederick Douglass. When he visited Brockport, he stayed with them. Anthony was active in the local Republican Party committee and in the "colored" Republican organization at the county level. He was one of two Sweden Republicans to attend the inauguration of President Garfield in 1881.

Williams was best known and most important for the work that she and her husband, Stephen Laing Williams, did in the area of civil rights. They were the principal representatives in the Midwest for Frederick Douglass and Booker T. Washington and, later, W. E. B. Du Bois. Through her association with Du Bois, she became one of the founders of the N.A.A.C.P. She was heavily involved in a number of civil rights activities, but, perhaps most importantly, in the African-American women's club movement, the main organization through which African-American women promoted the cause of racial equality.

Williams worked in the cause of civil rights through a great variety of activities. She engaged in a number of organizational projects. Besides the club movement, she was involved in a settlement house, a hospital, a nursing school, housing, education, employment, churches, and Republican Party politics. She also was a prolific writer in newspapers and magazines and a very popular traveling lecturer. She was a talented, trained musician, and sometimes accompanied her lectures on the piano. She was also an accomplished artist.

At a time when there was some rivalry and conflict between the activists promoting African-American and women's suffrage, Williams straddled both causes. She was a leader of the main suffragist organization in Illinois and was the only African-American invited to eulogize Susan B. Anthony at the National American Women's Suffrage Association convention in 1907. She wrote and spoke in support of the movement, including a talk to Brockport's W.C.T.U. on "Women's Mission" and "What Can She Do."

Clarina Nichols

Clarina Nichols was among those who swarmed from the east to Kansas in the late 1850s to join in the contest over the future of the territory. In 1854, Congress had enacted the Kansas-Nebraska bill based on Stephen A. Douglas's popular sovereignty principle that the citizens of those territories had the right to decide whether to be slave or free states. This led to a violent struggle between the two factions, called "Bloody Kansas." Nichols was a former Brockport resident who played an important role in Kansas becoming a free state.

She was born Clarina Irene Howard in West Townshend, Vt., in 1810, emigrated to Brockport with her husband, Justin Carpenter, in 1830, and launched her career as a social reformer. She and Justin became leaders in Brockport's temperance society, published a reformist weekly newspaper and a magazine, organized a lyceum and a lending library, and ran an elementary school.

By 1834, they had moved to New York City, where their marriage dissolved. Clarina returned to Vermont, remarried George Nichols and became the editor of the newspaper he published, which she used to promote women's rights and abolitionism. As a result of her efforts, both Vermont and New York granted women certain property rights. Also, she became a leader in the national women's rights movement as a delegate to several of their conventions and as a writer and a widely traveled lecturer, including in Brockport in 1856.

In 1854, she and her three sons emigrated to Kansas with a group of 225 Abolitionists, including the young Susan B. Anthony, whom Nichols mentored and became a close friend. In Kansas, she campaigned for women's rights and an anti-slavery constitution through her newspaper, as a lecturer, and by lobbying the constitutional convention. As a result of her efforts, the new Kansas constitution was the first in the Union to grant women equal educational rights, the vote in school district elections, equal child custody, and real and personal property rights. Two of her sons fought with John Brown's troops in Kansas, but did not go with him to Harper's Ferry. In 1871, she moved to California, where she died in 1885. Susan B. Anthony said of her, "No woman in so many varied fields of action has more steadily and faithfully labored" for the cause of women's rights.

Brockport Women

Brockport women in 1865 lived at a midpoint between the chartering of the village in 1829 and the end of the century. Brockport's population of 2,370 in 1865 included 1,230 women (51.9 percent), 449 of them in married couple households, 310 of which had their own children in the household. Thirty-six were female householders with no husband present, sixteen of them with their own children present. Household servants were more common in modest homes than now. Census data do not indicate which households with servants had female members, but thirty-seven of Brockport's households included servants. So at least a small percentage of housewives had resident hired help.

Thirty Brockport women owned land in 1865, twenty of whom were widows who, probably, inherited it from deceased husbands. Six of the thirty were single, two were married women not residing with their husbands, and two were married women residing with their husbands. So women, married or not, could legally own land, but not many did. Nearly ten times as many men (291) did.

Twenty-five women got married in 1865, all of them to men! Their average age was twenty-three and a half years, averaging seven years younger than their husbands. All of the brides were younger than the grooms. Two of the brides were widows, none were divorcees.

Although the overwhelming majority of Brockport's women in 1865 were housewives, at least ninety-two had gainful employment: seven as milliners, two "tailoresses", five school teachers, four dressmakers, forty-one maid servants, two telegraphers, one professional artist, one produce merchant, twenty-six in the clothing industry, and two were employed by a mitten and whip maker. In addition, of course, was the professional novelist, Mary Jane Holmes. That is 12.8 percent of the 715 females over the age of twenty. In 1855, women in the clothing industry earned $11–12 a month compared to $25 for men and in retail trade $6–7 to $30 for men.

Brockport's female population in 1865 was much less diverse racially than today's. Ten women and perhaps eight girls were African-American. No other females of a non-Caucasian race appear in Brockport's 1865 census.

Seven of the thirteen women who died in 1864–65 were victims of consumption (tuberculosis). This compared to only two of the seventeen men who died in that period. Two women died of diphtheria and one each of worms, typhoid fever, croup, and cancer. Apparently, none died in childbirth.

Politically, women were, certainly, second-class citizens, but they were not completely absent from the political process. The 1865 census lists two women as voters. One was a produce merchant. The other was a single woman with no occupation. A political activity in which women figured prominently was a rally celebrating Lincoln's victory in the 1860 election. The *Republic* reported that the audience was "composed half of each ladies and gentlemen." On the other hand, all of the elected officials were men. However, Brockport had a female postmistress, a patronage appointment, for some twenty years. Also, Susan B. Anthony and a female escaped slave made political speeches in Brockport during the 1860s.

Unlike in politics, women figured very importantly in the cultural and social life of the village; in fact, they seem to have dominated there. One small example: a favorite winter amusement of Brockporters was sleigh rides. One such excursion to Spencerport had seventy partyers, "of whom about two-thirds were ladies."

As landowners, occupationally, and politically, women in 1865 Brockport were present but a small minority. Socially and culturally, they seem to have ruled the roost.

4

Brockporters in the Military

The Militia

The militia unit was one of the most important organizations in early Brockport. Under state law, all able-bodied men, ages twenty-one to forty-five, were required to belong. Exceptions were made for members of the fire companies, others were exempt after ten years' service.

The post of commander of the unit was among the most prestigious in the community. Among the men who served in that position were Frederick Wilkie, son-in-law of Hiel Brockway; Robert Staples, who was elected supervisor of the Town of Sweden eleven times, more than any other man and also served in the State Assembly; and Davis Carpenter, another of Brockway's many sons-in-law, physician, and future congressman.

Militias were required by law to train at least one day a year. Company drills were held in June and general training in the fall, lasting from 9 a.m. until 6 p.m. The latter event seems to have been one of the highlights of the year in Brockport. Elisha Carpenter has left this description:

> General Training was by far the greatest event of all. The screeching fifes, and rattling tenor and booming bass drums, made music that surpassed anything I have ever heard since.... Battalion after battalion was drawn up in grand array. The commanding officers, with cocked hats, gilt epaulettes, buckskin gloves and red sashes, galloped up and down the line on richly caparisoned horses. After much time thus spent ... the stentorian voice of the commanding General [ordered] "Bat-tal-lion to the right!" The martial band struck up "The Girl I Left Behind

> Me"; the horses pranced and the grand march began. I was fairly lifted from my feet.

Another early resident described the uniforms: "[T]heir continental uniforms, swallow-tailed blue coats, brass buttons, grey pants, cockade hats with plumes of feathers, swords and belts for the officers and flint-lock muskets for the soldiers."

Another admirer, James Cornes, reflecting on boyhood experiences, described it this way:

> The three day officers' drill and the company drill on the first Monday in September did not attract particular attention, but when it was known that old general training was to take place, then look out; Nothing else was to be talked about or thought of until it was over.
>
> The morning was ushered in by the firing of musketry and commenced long before daybreak—the waking up of officers. No more sleep after that. So there was one day out of the three hundred and fifty that parents had not to call their sons in the morning. On such occasions we could go down to Clarkson by a short route through the woods. But we boys never availed ourselves of it, preferring to go around by way of Wilkies Corners to see the wagon loads of trainers coming down from the south. Their red and white plumes waving in the air, and occasionally a drum in sight would make every boy leap for joy.
>
> I remember Colonel Wilkie when he commanded a regiment in Clarkson. He was a fine-looking officer and, also, a strict disciplinarian, for I was near him one day when he put one of his captains under arrest. On this occasion the regiment was maneuvering in a huge field on the Forsyth farm west. Were we boys ever too late to see the regiment form we knew where to find it, at one of the following places: North on Deacon Palmer's place, near his old tannery, or south on Mr. Blodgett's field, or west on the Forsyth farm.—BR1/2/1890

Another account is less ecstatic, recounting the situation when the militia was withering:

> Guns were used, but only such as each soldier possessed. There were consequently a great variety, which were without doubt in all conditions—good, bad and indifferent. Toward the end of the militia's existence some who had not guns appeared with sticks such as they could secure and which would be apt to make the whole affair most ridiculous. No one except officers wore uniforms, and in the latter days the soldiers appeared in the most ridiculous costumes they could procure, making the parades a sort of fantastic drills.

Another critic described the decline of the militias this way:

> [Their] trainings were mere farces, so that they gradually fell into contempt, and finally into disuse.... Military organizations were not held in esteem; money and time expended in equipments and drill were considered thrown away; the fines imposed were insignificant in amount, and even these were seldom collected...

The last company drill was held in Brockport in 1840 or 1841. Thereafter, the militia system was replaced by the National Guard, formed of volunteers who were paid and organized in a much more professional way. The basic militia legislation remained in effect, permitting the conscription of all able-bodied men in time of war or insurrection. In fact, this was the basis of the mobilization of the Union Army in the Civil War. At that time, the National Guard consisted of 19,435 officers and men and the unorganized militia, subject to conscription, numbered 450,000 men.

Milo Starks

Milo Starks was Brockport's great Civil War hero. This essay recounts what he did to earn that reputation and offers an explanation as to how he came to have the personality and character that led him to perform those feats.

First, I shall describe his military career. Much of this comes from the chapter on the 140th New York Volunteer Infantry in my *Civil War Brockport* book. Also, I am grateful to Ashley Allen for permitting me to copy many of Starks's letters that he has. His home was that of the Starks family.

Starks's military career began in early August 1862 when he started recruiting men in Brockport for what became Company "A" in the 140th. He wound up with thirty-eight men from Clarkson, twenty from Sweden outside Brockport, eighteen from Brockport, eight from Hamlin, and fifteen from elsewhere, some of whom were Brockport Collegiate Institute students or *alumni*.

Starks was a single, twenty-six-year-old farmer, tall and dark, "with an intimidating appearance." At a farewell ceremony as the unit was leaving Rochester, Starks said that "his life was a stake laid down for the safety of the Republic, and should it be swept off in the grand game, he knew that those whom he left behind would feel proud that he died in his country's cause."

The 140th first saw battle at Fredericksburg but was at the periphery, and Company "A" suffered no casualties. At the Battle of Chancellorsville that followed, the 140th had one of the few successes in that Union disaster and three Company "A" men were wounded, one fatally.

The 140th and Starks in particular made their reputations at Gettysburg. As they marched past the rear slope of the Little Round Top hill to their appointed position, a general from another brigade confronted the regiment and ordered it to change course, climb the hill, and engage two Texas regiments that were ascending the opposite slope. The Texans would have outflanked the beleaguered 20th Maine and probably gained control of Little Round Top, which dominated the ground where the crucial battle was fought the following day.

Companies "A" and "G" led the regiment. In the confusion, they had not loaded their rifles or fixed their bayonets. However, the Texans did not know that and were confused when the Union troops suddenly loomed up before them. The rifles were loaded and a pitched battle ensued. Colonel O'Rorke, the regimental commander, was killed at the outset of the battle, leaving Starks, the captain of the lead company, in effective command of the regiment. The 140th repelled the Texans, saving Little Round Top. Starks was wounded four times, but refused to leave the battlefield until the fighting ended.

An officer in the 44th N.Y.V.I. who was involved in the battle listed seven officers who, he believed, had saved Little Round Top that day—three generals, two colonels, an artillery lieutenant, and Starks. Historian Allan Nevins called the retention of Little Round Top "pivotal to the Union victory on [July] third."

Starks's performance is the more remarkable in view of the state of his health. Twelve days before the crucial battle, Starks wrote home:

> For several days, I had felt quite unwell and after two days march was completely used up. The first 25 miles I carried one of my boys knapsacks in addition to my own load.... I came near having a sunstroke.... After reaching camp my head ached so badly that after noon and the next day I could not sit up.... My health has not been very good since the Chancellorsville march. I have been very bilious and now the doctor says my liver and kidneys are quite a good deal affected.

The 140th saw no more conflict until May 5, 1864, in the Battle of Saunders Field. This was a disaster for the 140th: Company "A" lost twenty-one of its remaining fifty-three men, killed, wounded, or captured. Starks narrowly escaped.

At the Battle of Laurel Hill on May 10, the 140th attacked an entrenched Confederate force twice and was repulsed. As they reached within three rods of the enemy on a third attempt, Colonel Ryan, the regimental commander, was killed. Starks had been promoted to major and became Ryan's successor. He dismounted and was trying to lead the regiment on foot, when a bullet struck him in the forehead, killing him instantly.

Some idea of the esteem with which the men of Company "A" regarded their commander may be gained from some of Starks's letters. Before Gettysburg, he wrote: "I hope my health and strength will be spared to me to see my noble little band through this wicked strife. I believe they will follow any where I may be called to go and that without a murmur."

That was certainly the case at Gettysburg. His men were exhausted after an arduous two-week forced march. Many were barefoot. Yet one soldier wrote: "You had ought to have seen our boys fight ... nothing could exceed their bravery. They charged and re-charged, never being in any instance repelled." Historian Bruce Catton called their charge "as strange a counterattack as the army ever saw ... they simply ran straight at their foes, and the only weight the charge had was the weight of their running bodies."

In a letter home, Starks says, "Several times the Col. has said he wished the other Captains could get along as nicely with their companies as I did with mine." When he returned to the company from a furlough, "My men seemed very much pleased to see me return and gave me a hearty welcome." Another letter suggests why they had such respect for him. He wrote:

> I have so many letters to answer from parents & friends of my company that I am very busy. Of late I have sent from four to six per day. Each one seems so anxious to [know] the whereabouts of their son & think I can do so much for them. I sometimes feel quite discouraged & yet I take a comfort in giving to each one all the information possible.

One characteristic that seems to have prepared Starks for his heroic role was his talent as a natural leader. His father was so preoccupied with his work for the Baptists that he left management of the farm to Milo, even though he was the fourth eldest son. George, the eldest, had decamped to Oregon; Cyrus had also left the farm; and Maurice deferred to Milo, though he was three years his elder.

Milo was a very enterprising farmer. He got the family engaged in fruit raising and sold fruit trees as an itinerant peddler in Michigan, Illinois, and Iowa. While engaged in that way, he wrote to Maurice frequently, instructing him on running the farm. He continued to do so while in the army, and Maurice responded by seeking Milo's advice.

One example of his instructions to Maurice is in a letter from Iowa in 1862: "Morris if you ... will take care of the old farm for me I will pay you well for it. I should wish you to go on there not as a common hired man but as if the thing was your own and to act accordingly."

Beyond his natural leadership qualities, Milo's character was largely defined by his devout Baptist faith. His grandfather was reputed to have been deeply religious and his father devoted his life to serving the Baptist church. Israel made his living as an itinerant peddler of Baptist books and served during the war as a volunteer in the U.S. Christian Commission tending the wounded.

In 1841, Israel had moved his family from Leroy and bought a farm just south of Brockport in order to revive Brockport's Baptist church, which had been dissolved and its building foreclosed. E. M. Kniffen, in a history of the church, says: "[U]ndoubtedly it was the interest and the untiring energy of Deacon Israel Starks ... that made the success of the newly organized church possible."

Maurice, too, was a devout Baptist and a leader in the local temperance organization. He was a deacon, the church clerk in 1871–83, and the Sunday school

Congressman Henry W. Seymour.

Druggist Thomas H. Dobson.

Left: Attorney Henry Rogers Selden.

Below: Inventor George B. Selden with his 1906 automobile.

Congressman Elias Holmes.

Traveler Burton Holmes.

Above: William H. Seymour (above) and Dayton S. Morgan. Upper right shows a foundry like theirs. (*Detail from Portraits of Our Past mural by Rick Muto*)

Left: Gifford Morgan, Dayton's youngest son.

Brockport Republic publisher Horatio N. Beach.

Brockport Republic/Brockport Republic-Democrat publisher Peter A. Blossom.

Inventor Samuel Johnston of Johnston Harvester Co.

Merchant Tailor Edward Harrison.

John Ostrom, builder of the Morgan-Manning House.

Charles B. Greenough.

Above: Taxidermist Carl Ethan Akeley.

Left: Congressman Richard Cutts Shannon.

Right: John Hall Deane. (*Photo from Rare Books, Special Collections and Preservation, River Campus Libraries, University of Rochester*)

Below: Mortar schooner *John Smith*. Same class as one on which Deane served.

Above: School Commissioner Fred W. Hill.

Left: George Guelph, photographer, taxidermist, printer.

Photographer John H. Kent.

Frederick P. Root, wife, and farm home. (*From History of Monroe County, 1877*)

Above: Mary Jane Holmes at desk and Fannie Barrier Williams. (*Detail from Portraits of Our Past mural by Rick Muto*)

Below: Porter Hotel building.

Above: World War I enlistment parade.

Right: World War I Home Guard patrol.

Old Home Week souvenir postcard.

Brockport Fair horse race.

Above: Brockport Freezers N.Y.S. baseball champs.

Right: Brockport's Seth Thomas tower clock.

Left: Frederick Douglass, portrait by John Kent.

Below: The village board that proposed urban renewal. (*From Town of Sweden Sesqui-Centennial Celebration*)

superintendent in 1876–85. In 1894, he led a group of nineteen members to withdraw from the church and form the Emmanuel Baptist Church. A year later, they had sixty-nine members and Maurice was a deacon and Sunday school superintendent. The defectors returned to the First Baptist Church by 1904 and Maurice was on its Executive Committee and a Sunday school teacher. He frequently ran, always unsuccessfully, for public office on the Prohibition Party ticket.

In the context of the religious devotion of his family, it is easy to see why Milo was similarly committed. His feelings are reflected in many of his letters. He wrote to one of his sisters: "[M]y prayer is that you may become one of his devoted followers, that when parting is known no more we may meet in that blest abode which he hath gone to prepare." After the Battle of Saunders Field, he wrote home: "By the kindness of a kind Providence my life and health are still spared." In a letter to Maurice, he wrote: "[O]ne sometimes ... longs for the quiet home Sabbath where he can sit quietly & read or write or meditate unmolested." In another, he wrote: "As a people we have been sinful & until these are atoned for no doubt we will be kept in trouble & suspense until those sins are wiped away."

I could quote many more such comments, but I believe those adequately support my conclusion, which is that Milo Starks's innate sense of how to inspire and lead men in even the most difficult and perilous situations and his profound faith in the protective power of a benevolent God account for his heroic conduct in the Union Army.

James S. Lowery

James S. Lowery was born in Rochester, one of six children, whose ages were nine to twenty-eight in 1862. His mother was an Irish-born widow and he was a Clarkson farm boy when he enlisted. He was a collateral ancestor of Erwin Duryea, probably Duryea's great-great grand uncle. Marilyn Duryea has two of his wartime diaries, which she kindly allowed me to transcribe. Lowery was twenty-five years old when he enlisted, and he was 5 feet 8 inches tall with a light complexion, blond hair, and blue eyes.

Lowery enlisted on August 7, 1862, in Company "A" of the 140th N.Y.V.I., the Brockport unit whose commander was Capt. Milo Starks. He was with his regiment in the disastrous Battle of Chancellorsville on May 5, 1863, and the successful Battle of Gettysburg on July 2–3, 1863, when the 140th played a decisive role in the defense of Little Round Top. His diary says merely, "Started to march at 4 a.m. march about three hours when we formed line of battle. About 5 p.m. we move up to our left & was soon engaged. We had 6 men killed & 5 wounded. Our Col. Was killed also Capt."

Lowery complained frequently in his diary of "horrible" headaches, "dreadful" coughing, "very sore throat," and toothaches. He may have been suffering from tuberculosis. He also complained often of being tired, cold and wet in the winter, and of the heat, even as early as April.

He was captured on May 5, 1864, during the Battle of the Wilderness, one of five officers and ninety-six enlisted men who were captured during that three-day battle. His diary entry for that day reads simply: "Reveille at 4 a.m. all packed up ready to march 12 M formed line of battle & advance about 1 mile halted & sent out skirmishers then the whole line advanced met the enemy I was taken prisoner and marched to "Orange Court House" under guard." The prisoners were shipped for "a hideous ride of 93 miles" by cattle car to Lynchburg to join about 15,000 other "Yank Prisoners," then on to Dansville, Virginia, on the 11th, and, finally, underwent a six-day trip by rail to Andersonville, Georgia, arriving on the 24th.

While a prisoner, he complained frequently of not having anything or very little to eat. Typical diary entries: "... breakfast of corn bread & cold muddy water out of the Dan River," "very tired and lonesome," "was sick all night," "cold & hungry & nothing to eat," "I was almost suffocated in the cars last night," "My head aches awfully," "O this is a horrid place for any human being to live in," "I went down to the Run & washed my clothes I used sand as a substitute for soap," "about 30 [prisoners] die every night," "I can hardly walk I am so weak ... I tried to cut a piece of [hard tack] but could not," "my dihoreaha [*sic.*] is running into the dysentery." He frequently reported having read the Bible.

On June 26, 1864, he wrote: "... the rumor is that they are going to parole the sick tomorrow." On Sunday, June 27, the diary's last entry says, "James is worse this p.m. and wants me to take charge of his things at 20 minutes to 10 he says tell mother I died for my country and trusted in God—James S. Lowery died this p.m. 20 minutes to 4 p.m."

Lowery spent twenty-one months in the 140th, being sick and miserable most of the time, fighting in several pitched battles, and seeing many of his comrades killed or wounded. He then spent fifty-two days slowly starving to death in execrable conditions, dying on the day he had hoped to be paroled. Such was the glamor and glory of war for James S. Lowery, the farm boy from Clarkson.

John Tyler Farnham

John Tyler Farnham wrote the remarkable diaries that form my book *The Life of a Union Army Sharpshooter*, which had a complicated genesis. While writing the section on the 1860–65 period of my *Early Brockport* book, I discovered some 189 letters from Brockport soldiers in the Union Army that were published in the *Brockport Republic* during the war. I thought that they might be the basis for another book, so I omitted any material on the village's involvement in the Civil War from *Early Brockport*. However, when I tried to use those letters to form a cohesive narrative, I found that they did not lend themselves to such use. But the forty-eight extant letters by John T. Farnham in the *Brockport Republic* seemed a possibility by themselves.

On a whim, I Googled "John T. Farnham" and learned that five of his wartime diaries were held by the Wichita State University Library. I traveled to Wichita twice and transcribed those diaries. Then, I Googled him again and learned that a sixth diary of his had been sold at auction the previous November for $23,900. It had been accompanied by a blood-stained shirt cuff that had been taken from the body of the assassinated Abraham Lincoln. A diary entry explained how Farnham had acquired the shirt cuff. I called the auction house, left a message, and wrote a letter asking that they let the buyer know that I would like to transcribe the diary. I received no answer from either my phone call or my letter.

The very next week, the *New York Times* ran an article about a Jewish physician named John Lattimer who had collected Nazi memorabilia and whose estate had been sold at auction. It also mentioned that he had collected Lincoln memorabilia, including the Farnham diary, and gave the name of Lattimer's daughter who was the executor and lived in Topeka, Kans. I called her, left a message, wrote her a letter, enclosing another letter to the buyer of the diary, asking her to forward it to the buyer. In the buyer's letter, I offered to transcribe the diary for him and collaborate with him in any way he wished. Again, no answers.

Again, I Googled Farnham. This time, I learned that the sixth diary and the shirt cuff had been displayed as part of an exhibit honoring the bicentennial of Abraham Lincoln's birth at the Herbert Hoover Memorial Library in West Branch, Ia., in 2009 and that it belonged to Dr. Blaine V. Houmes, of Cedar Rapids, Ia. I called Dr. Houmes and left a message. I wrote him a long letter, offering to come to Cedar Rapids and transcribe the diary. No answer. Six weeks later, I was standing in my pantry when my cellphone rang and Dr. Houmes told me that I would not need to come to Iowa. He would copy the diary for me and send me the copy. He did and the result is part of my book *The Life of a Union Army Sharpshooter*.

Incidentally, I was able to return a favor to Dr. Houmes. He asked my help in identifying the friend of Farnham who had given him the shirt cuff. I did some research in the local history department of Rundell Library, found out who she was, and let Dr. Houmes know.

Nathan P. Pond

Nathan P. Pond was born and reared on Brockport's Mechanic Street (now Park Avenue) as the son of Levi Pond, a prominent business and civic leader, including membership in the N.Y.S. Assembly. Nathan was in the lumber business at the outbreak of the Civil War. In August 1862, he recruited and organized Company "M" of the 3rd New York Cavalry regiment. That regiment had one of the longest lists of engagements of any in the Union Army—126. They were mostly raids. It had an exceptionally high casualty rate, with 308 killed or wounded, including forty-six officers and men killed or died of wounds. In January 1864, Pond transferred to the 3rd U.S. Colored Cavalry regiment as a lieutenant colonel and second in command. He served in that capacity until the end of the war. After the war, he was a harbormaster in Brockport, but by 1870, he had moved to Rochester where he and a partner founded the *Democrat & Chronicle*, which he owned until his death at eighty-eight years old in 1921.

Stephen Randall Stafford

Stephen Randall Stafford was born in Stafford, N.Y., but was reared in a house on the southeast corner of College and Utica Streets that still stands, the son of a faculty member at the Collegiate Institute. He enlisted in the 13th N.Y.V.I. regiment on April 30, 1861, fifteen days after the firing on Fort Sumter, but was discharged on September 18 "for minority," although he was eighteen years old. However, on August 17, 1862, he was commissioned a second lieutenant in the 129th N.Y.V.I., which became the 8th N.Y. Heavy Artillery regiment. He was promoted to first lieutenant on January 27, 1864, to captain on November 5, 1864, and to "major, by brevet, for faithful and meritorious services during the war" on March 13, 1865. He had been wounded in May 1864, but led "a desperate charge at Hatcher's Run on October 27, 1864, for which General Gibbon—his divisional commander—tendered him high praise and honor in the presence of the entire command." After the war, he became a professional officer, fought in the Indian wars, and commanded Fort Sheridan. He retired in 1898 for physical disability and returned to Brockport, where he engaged in the insurance business. He died at his desk on May 31, 1902.

Morton A. Read

Morton A. Read was born and grew up in Brockport. His father, Resolved, was a carpenter and Morton was a printer. He enlisted in the 8th New York Cavalry as a private on October 14, 1861, giving his age as eighteen, though in the 1860 census, his age is fourteen. He became a corporal on June 16, 1863, sergeant on August 1, 1863, first sergeant on April 9, 1864, and was commissioned a first lieutenant on February 6, 1865. He was awarded the Congressional Medal of Honor for having captured the battle flag of the 1st Texas Infantry regiment at the Battle of Appomattox Station on April 8, 1865. The capture of the battle flag of an enemy unit was considered an especially heroic feat because a unit's battle flag was its rallying point. To capture such a flag threatened to throw the enemy into disarray and destroy its cohesion as a fighting force. As the battle flag held the central position in the unit, its bearer was, at least theoretically, in the least vulnerable location. After the war, Read moved to Cincinnati. However, his son, Morton G., returned to Brockport. The architect, Edwin Read, who lived in the house on Main Street next to the Morgan Manning House, was Morton A.'s grandson.

The Spanish-American War

The Spanish-American War began in the aftermath of the sinking of the battleship *Maine* in Havana harbor on February 15, 1898. War broke out on April 23. Only on April 28 did the *Brockport Republic* notice the developing crisis, and even then, it simply predicted: "Unless a miracle intervenes ... the United States and Spain will be at war on Saturday (April 30) or at the latest on Sunday" and "With firm confidence in the justice of their cause and in the favor of the Almighty, the American Nation awaits the conflict."

With the passage of thirty-three years since the Civil War ended, the memories of the horrors of that conflict had faded and been replaced by those of heroism and glory. Brockport, like the rest of the nation, was eager for another opportunity to express its patriotism and bravery in a just cause—which Cuban freedom seemed to be.

Brockport first expressed its support for the war when a company of volunteers from Medina passed through the village by train on May 2 and were greeted by "a very large crowd, headed by the band and local G.A.R.... Cheer after cheer went up from their throats.... One old man ... yelled ... 'Them ---- Spaniards won't dare look such an honest lot of boys in the face.'"

In early June, twelve Brockport boys went to Medina to enlist. Three failed the second medical exam and three others did not take it. The remaining six were sworn in on June 15. One other Brockporter served in the war, but the *Republic* mentioned him only when he was suffering from malaria.

On June 20, seven Brockport boys left for Camp Alger, their training camp in Virginia, arriving the next day:

> Nearly 500 people assembled at the depot ... to do honor to the boys.... The band was present and when the train came in played several selections, cannons were fired and the air rang with shouts for the soldier boys [one of whom] waving the American flag, was seized by the crowd and pulled through the car window and quickly raised upon their shoulders, while three rousing cheers were given.

From May 19, the *Republic* ran long letters from soldiers on their experiences traveling to and living in training camps. Brockport recruit Fred E. Gladwin, a Normal School student, wrote four letters to the *Republic* from Camp Alger. The conditions in camp were miserable. It was hot, humid, and crowded, "a breeding place for disease." Malaria and typhoid fever were epidemic. Two of the seven Brockport soldiers were among those afflicted. Life in the camp was pretty dull, and it was relieved only by excursions to nearby sites.

The home front seems to have been involved in the war in two ways. First, by responding to the appeal launched by the *Republic* for donations to a "National

Relief Fund" to be expended by the Red Cross Society and the Central Cuban Relief Committee. Every donor of at least $1 would receive "a copy of the beautiful picture, 'The Accolade.'" Second, by sending packages of food and clothing to the boys in training camp, whose receipt Gladwin acknowledges.

Sixteen members of the local post of the Grand Army of the Republic, Civil War veterans, volunteered to serve as a kind of home guard "to assist in the enforcement of the law, the suppression of insurrection, and to repel invasion" in New York State during the war.

The war ended on August 12, before the Brockport boys had completed their training. A "Union Thanksgiving service for peace" was held in the Presbyterian Church on the 14th. Six Brockport soldiers arrived home on September 13. One was still on sick call. Their company received a tumultuous welcome in Medina, where it had been formed, and the Brockporters were similarly welcomed when they arrived home. The *Republic* commented: "That our boys did not see active service during the war detracted not at all from the enthusiasm of their welcome." The reality was that the war had ended for Brockport more with a whimper than a roar—no glory, but also no gore.

The U.S. 9th Infantry Regiment

The U.S. 9th Infantry Regiment included twelve young Brockport men in its campaigns combatting the insurrection in the Philippines that followed the Spanish-American War and in the Boxer Rebellion in China of 1899–1901.

Two of the seven Brockporters who had served in the 3rd N.Y.V.I. during the Spanish-American War joined ten other young Brockporters in the 9th U.S. Infantry Regiment, a Regular Army unit, and fought in the Philippines and China. Apparently, the other ten had already served in Cuba, for the *Brockport Republic* said that they had "fought Spaniards, Phillippinos and Chinese and traveled from east to west 10,000 miles."

In Cuba, the 9th Infantry helped capture San Juan Hill, leading to the occupation of the city of Santiago and the end of the hostilities in Cuba. Colonel Theodore Roosevelt and his Rough Riders captured the public imagination for their role in that battle. Little noted was the part played by four infantry regiments, including the 9th, and five other cavalry regiments. The 9th lost one officer and four enlisted men killed and twenty-seven enlisted men wounded, one dying later. No Brockporters were among the casualties.

Following the Cuban campaign, the 9th returned to its home base near Sackett's Harbor, N.Y. Due to discharges for disability and other factors, it was 900 men under strength. Then, on February 1, 1899, insurgents rose up against the American occupation of the Philippines. On March 3, the 9th was ordered to leave for that theater of operations and, therefore, needed to refill its ranks by recruitment. Brockporters John Ross and Joseph Allen probably were among the 127 recruited in Rochester or the eight in Medina.

The 9th was much more active in the Philippines than it had been in Cuba. From May 17, 1899, until March 13, 1900, it took part in thirty-three armed engagements. Then, between July 13 and August 24, 1900, it fought six times in the multi-national effort to end the Boxer Rebellion in China. Finally, between June 30, 1901, and February 16, 1902, it was back in the Philippines, where it fought in another thirty-three operations.

At least six letters from the Brockport boys were published in the *Brockport Republic*. One of them recounted the July 1900 operation to capture the Chinese city of Tientsin in which American, Japanese, Russian, German, French, and English troops were engaged, including Brockporters Frank Fitzgerald and Frank Jinks. Others described armed action against the Filipino insurrectionaries. One of the Brockporters, Edwin R. Riley, died of malaria. All the others returned safely, some of them after almost four years of service.

World War I

World War I did not involve Brockporters as much as had the Civil War, neither in intensity nor duration. The home front was not as heavily committed nor did as large a proportion of young men serve in the military. American involvement lasted only eighteen months, compared to four years in the Civil War. Nevertheless, its war-related activities were substantial.

The *Brockport Republic* published news about the war extensively from its beginning, and when U.S. entry seemed imminent, it began to give much coverage to local war-related activities, rallying its readers to the "patriotic cause."

On March 29, 1917, it published a "Declaration" passed by the village board to declare "my absolute loyalty to the Government of the United States and pledge my support to you in any steps which you may take to protect American rights against unlawful violence upon land and sea, in guarding the Nation against hostile attacks and in upholding international law." Three weeks later, it reported that Mayor Harmon had received a letter from President Wilson's secretary, saying that "The President is greatly cheered and heartened" by the Declaration.

The home front activities related to the war were much different from those during the Civil War. Brockporters did not undertake some of the major Civil War efforts. They did not hold "war meetings" to recruit companies. In fact, they were very little engaged in recruitment efforts. Nor did they raise money for bonus payments.

Nevertheless, the home front undertook a substantial number of activities supporting the war. A very early one was promoting the growing of gardens to produce the food that was believed to be in short supply to feed the army that was expected to be "almost a million men ... by September." That effort was the subject of a "Mass Meeting at Grange Hall," called at "the request of the Governor and of the State Grange ... to discuss the serious food problem confronting our country." Similarly, the community was urged to go meatless and heatless one day a week and to use oleomargarine instead of butter.

A Brockport chapter of the American Red Cross was organized already on March 19, 1917, to support its parent organization's work to "relieve pain, to care for the wounded and dying" at the battle front. By April 19, it had "about 65" members and was recruiting more members and cash donations. Membership in the local chapter cost "$1.00, half of which goes to the National Body." By June 21, $1,400 had been donated by forty-seven men. Its financial report for November 1917 showed $129.46 in donations and $59.18 in expenditures. A week-long membership drive in late December produced more than 1,000 new members. By October 1918, the local chapter had sent fifteen boxes and barrels of clothing "for Belgian sufferers" and was soliciting another 100 pairs of pajamas, bath towels, hand towels, handkerchiefs, and napkins.

The Y.M.C.A. chapter was another local organization supporting the war effort. It participated in a drive to raise funds for the war work of its parent organization. The first day of the drive produced $600 of the $2,500 goal. A Rochester attorney who had visited Camp Dix where a number of Brockport boys were in training described for a public meeting the many services the Y.M.C.A. provided. In May 1918, a member of the Normal School faculty was selected to join the Y.M.C.A. as a "canteen worker" in France.

An *ad hoc* "War Relief Committee" was formed under the auspices of the D.A.R. It sent packages of fruit, candy, and tobacco through the Red Cross to Brockport boys in the training camps. In October, the *Republic* published letters from nine Brockport soldiers at Camp Dix and thirteen of them at Camp Wadsworth expressing their thanks for such packages. The committee included a "Knitting Committee" that, by late December 1917, had shipped to Brockport boys in the camps 270 sweaters, 228 scarfs, 241 pairs of wristlets, 108 pairs of socks, and three helmets. A "Gauze Work Committee" produced "hospital dressings." In May 1918, the committee began a "War Chest Fund," asking "each citizen to pledge a percentage of his yearly income to a fund which will meet the needs of war relief work." Its "Woman's Committee" sold $147,450 worth of Liberty Loans in the fourth drive.

The Boy Scouts contributed to the war effort. A good part of the success of the drive to sell Liberty Loans was credited to Boy Scouts. Also, they met April 30, 1917, to discuss the "feasibility of gardening on a large scale" and a committee was "appointed with power to act." They distributed "Government literature of all kinds, including war pamphlets, Red Cross and W.S.S., posters; they sold Red Cross stamps and secured Red Cross subscriptions; the collection of Books for soldiers and sailors, the cultivation of war-gardens ... and many other collective services."

Not to be outdone by the boys, the Girl Patriots, numbering "about fifty" members, participated in the parades for departing soldiers and also met every week to knit "the various articles which are in such great demand for our boys."

On April 26, 1917, the First National Bank published an advertisement in the *Republic* announcing that the "United States Government will shortly issue a war loan which will probably be the largest ever offered in this country." The bank promised to "furnish you the official details as soon as they are available and will be glad to handle subscriptions without profit or commission of any kind." The first Liberty Loan drive in October 1917 produced $218,000 for Sweden, Clarkson, and Hamlin. The Brockport–Clarkson–Hamlin District oversubscribed its fourth Liberty Loan goal of $381,600 by "about $46,000," with Brockport accounting for $282,150.

In late May 1917, the Brockport Home Defense League was organized with the cooperation of "the churches, patriotic and social organization, G.A.R., Boy Scouts, Sons of Veterans and many clubs." It called a meeting that was "awakening great enthusiasm in the community." "M. Jean A. Picard, the famous French soldier" spoke to the meeting about his experiences as a frontline soldier in the war. "T.C. Gordon ... gave a brief sketch of the work of the home defense league." "Dr. John M. Swan, director of the Rochester Base Hospital" spoke on "the preparations made to care for wounded men." "Everyone in Brockport and the neighboring villages and county [was] urged to avail themselves of this opportunity to learn of this war." By June 1, "upwards of 50 citizens ... signed the enrollment list."

In October 1917, New York Guard and Depot Units were added to the Home Defense League. Members were to be armed and uniformed by the state and be prepared to serve on guard duty anywhere in the state. By late November, it had seventy members. Members of the League unwilling to stand guard duty were to be placed in a Home Defense Reserve. Every Thursday evening, the Home Defense League drilled on Main Street from 7 to 9 p.m., with Dr. John Hazen as commander-in-chief.

Even such social clubs as the "Junior Birthday Club" got into the war effort. Its members spent "most" of one afternoon in early May 1917 "making up comfort packets for the soldiers in the trenches of France"—never mind that no American soldiers were anywhere near such trenches.

The Normal School also got heavily involved in war-related activities. It greeted American entry in the war with "patriotic exercises ... as an expression of the loyalty of the students to the government." In late May, it followed up by celebrating a "France Day" in compliance with "the concurrent resolution of the Legislature, the Governor's proclamation, and the direction of Dr. Finley, State Commissioner of Education."

In October 1917, the State Military Training Commission offered the Normal School the opportunity to host a military training program if sixteen or more students or community members, aged sixteen to nineteen, signed up. Additionally, the Normal School library offered to forward to soldiers in training or "in the trenches and in the hospitals" any books donated for that purpose.

Charles D. Cooper, superintendent of the Training Department of the Normal School, served as a civilian in the War Camp Community Service for the War Department and Navy Department Commissions on Training Camp Activities. That organization was charged with "stimulating and aiding communities in the neighborhood of training camps to develop and organize their social and recreational resources in such a way as to be of the greatest possible value to the officers and soldiers in the camps."

Apparently, rumors circulated in the community that Rev. H. F. Wind, a Lutheran chaplain in the Marines, was guilty of "disloyal remarks or disloyal actions," for he published a letter in the *Republic* in early June 1918 denying them and "a patriotic meeting" was held in the Strand Theater supporting him.

In addition to the many war-related activities on the home front, of course, many Brockporters did military service. Even before American entry, two young Brockport women were in France, volunteering for nursing duty with the French military. Also, several Brockporters had enlisted in the "mosquito coast defense patrol."

On May 10, 1917, the *Republic* reported: "There is no chance of Brockporter's being accused of showing the slacker spirit with the long list of men [seventeen] who have enlisted so far from this village." They included service in the "Hospital division," the "Reserve Coast Defense ... the company of Dental Surgeons ... the National Defense Committee ... the Engineers Officers' Reserve Corps, [and] the Officers' Reserve Corps." Another early enlistment was with the American Red Cross. Nearly every issue thereafter added names to its list.

The draft that had been the backup for the recruitment efforts in the Civil War was reinstituted in May 1917 and the *Republic* provided details in its May 24 edition. All men, aged twenty-one to forty-five, were required to register on June 5. They were numbered in the order of their registration. That information was forwarded to Washington, where the drawing for call-up order was made. Sweden registered 288 men, Hamlin 172, and Clarkson ninety-four.

The seven-town district that included Sweden had a quota of 175 men and Hamlin's district had 198. Twice as many were called for physical exams as were to be drafted. The examiners, working in the Normal School building, examined thirty-seven Brockport men. Twenty-nine were deemed fit, including eighteen who claimed an exemption. Seven failed the physical and one enlisted. That record makes one wonder about the absence of "slacker spirit" among Brockport men. Another twenty-eight Brockporters were called up for examinations on September 22, four more on January 5, 1918, another seventy-one on February 25, six more on April 3, and eight on May 27, 1918. The September draft call enlisted ten Brockporters.

On September 7, nine draftees from the district, including three Brockporters (Howard Brule, Howard Bulmore, and Francis Burch), left the village by train for "a southern training camp." The townspeople gave them a rousing sendoff. The schools were closed. A parade to the train station included the mayor, the trustees, the district attorney, "Soldier Boys in automobiles," members of the G.A.R., the Brockport Drum Corps, Boy Scouts, "Girl Patriots," and "Citizens in automobiles." A "thousand people" at the train station heard the mayor and the head of the Exemption Board praise the "brave young men" and "scathingly score the slackers." As the train pulled out, the band played the national anthem and "the Girl Patriots showered the boys with flowers."

Another ten men "known in this village" had left the previous Friday for service in the Second Ambulance Corps, ten more draftees shipped out on September 27, and another twenty-seven in November. Each time, they were honored by a "rousing" sendoff, including the usual parade. A total of 165 men from Sweden, Clarkson, and Hamlin were drafted. By July 1918, the *Republic* published a list of 138 Brockporters and twenty-five former residents "or whose parents reside[d]" there who were serving in the military. Four more shipped out on July 26. Another four Brockporters had joined the merchant marine.

In late December, Brockport men of draft age were receiving questionnaires from the Selective Service Administration. Their answers were intended to identify men who should be drafted. A three-member committee of local men was appointed to help the boys complete the forms.

A National Guard company of "about 80" men was based in Brockport. Three of its members left for "Federal service" in March 1918.

On December 20, the *Republic* ran a list of seventy-four men serving in the military from the Brockport area. It cautioned that it was probably incomplete and may contain the names of boys from other towns. In January 1919, the *Republic* published a list of ninety-five Normal School students and graduates who had served in the military during the war.

In December 1918, the *Republic* announced that funds were being solicited to buy a "service flag" to be hung over Main Street honoring Brockport's servicemen. On January 5, 1918, the flag was presented to the village president to the accompaniment of music by the Brockport band. The Normal School was planning a similar flag with a star for each of its students who had entered the service. The Masonic Lodge also hoisted a flag, with eleven stars representing the members of the lodge who were serving in the military.

In May 1918, physician Horace J. Mann received a commission in the Medical Reserve Corps of the army as a captain.

On May 17, the *Republic* published the first two of many, many letters from Brockport soldiers. One boy was in the 4th N.Y. Infantry, the other in the 8th N.Y. Cavalry, both in training in Texas. Almost every issue thereafter carried at least one letter from a soldier.

By late November 1917, the first of Brockport's soldier boys had arrived in France. The first known war casualty to affect the Brockport community was the battlefield death of a Normal School student from East Rochester in mid-April 1918. On May 29, 1918, Charles Harsh, a former Normal School student and Brockport resident, was killed in battlefield action in Cantigny, France. He had enlisted on May 1, 1917, and shipped to France with the first American regiment to arrive there on July 1, 1917. In August 1918, two Brockport soldiers were wounded, one in the Battle of Belleau Woods and the other after Chateau Thierry, and another was listed among the missing. On September 15, 1918, Edward Seaman of Hamlin was killed at Saint-Michel, France. Brockporter Arthur Crisp "died of wounds" at Thiaucourt, France on September 20, 1918. Four other Brockporters, Ira and Lester Cooley, Thomas Palmer, and Myron Whitlock died of the flu stateside in October 1918.

One Brockport soldier was "cited for bravery in action." Two ambulance drivers were cited for bravery, one received the *Croix de Guerre* from the Italian government for having evacuated 204 wounded Italians "in the face of heavy shell fire at one period for two days and nights without cessation" and the other "for devotion to duty in the evacuation of wounded over heavily shelled roads in the battle of the Hindenburg Line." Seven Brockporters were awarded the Purple Heart.

One Brockporter, John Hyland, enlisted as a private, stayed in the army after the war, and served in World War II as a lieutenant-colonel.

5

Brockport's Economy

Manufacturing in Brockport

Between 1866 and 1916, the United States underwent what economists call a Second Industrial Revolution. Brockport participated fully in that phenomenon. In effect, the nation was industrialized—and so was Brockport.

Nationwide, the number of manufacturing establishments doubled between 1858 and 1914. The number of workers in manufacturing nearly tripled and the value of manufactured products grew 6.7 times between 1869 and 1916. The United States became a modern industrial nation.

Brockport became a modern industrial community during much the same period. Actually, its industrialization began well before 1866. A shop manufacturing carriages opened in 1822, the year the village was laid out. By the early 1830s, a Brockport firm was manufacturing threshing machines. The 1845 state census reported that $19,000 worth of manufactured goods had been produced in Brockport that year. Manufacturing became the most important element in the economy of the village with the production of reapers in 1846.

Farm implements were Brockport's most important manufactured products. The Seymour & Morgan foundry led the way with the production of the first 100 McCormick reapers. It became Dayton S. Morgan & Co. with the retirement of William Seymour in 1877 and ceased business about 1894 after Morgan's death in 1890. Brockport had several other farm implement factories. For instance, in the 1860s, it had Silliman Bro. & Co., Stevens & Holmes, Whiteside & Barnett, William Bradford and his bean planter, and the Johnston Harvester Co., besides Morgan. Also, Henry Seymour, son of William, produced reapers in a building across the street from his father's plant. The Johnston Harvester Co. on North Main Street was, at one time, the largest factory in Monroe County until it burned in 1882 and moved to Batavia.

Other manufacturers in Brockport have produced clocks, boxes, galvanized metal products, pianos, piano boxes, all sorts of processed foods, wagon and carriage wheels, fishing tackle, refrigerating appliances, shoes, dolls, and even two automobiles. The largest of Brockport's manufacturers, however, were the post-World War II General Electric Co. small appliance plant and the Owens-Illinois bottle works. Their closing in the 1980s brought Brockport's status as an industrial center to a close.

The Brockport Republic

The *Brockport Republic* became Brockport's weekly newspaper in 1856, with Horatio Beach as editor and publisher. In 1870, the *Brockport Democrat* began. In about 1877, Horatio turned over effective management of the paper to his son, Lorenzo, though he remained active as its "political editor." In 1896, Beach died. Lorenzo died in December 1897 and was succeeded by his wife, Nellie S. Beach. On January 1, 1899, Peter A. Blossom, a school teacher and administrator, bought the paper and was its editor and proprietor for fifty-five years and publisher for all but the final three years, when Richard Cross had that title.

During Blossom's tenure, he merged it with the *Democrat* in 1925. The *Brockport Republic-Democrat* ceased publication in 1972. For over a century, they were a window on their world for Brockporters. This essay will peek through the *Republic* in November 1914 as a window to see how the world looked to Brockporters at that time.

The *Republic* reported on all of the big happenings in the community. For instance, in November 1914, it reported that the Monitor Clock Co. was the newest Brockport industry, it announced the election returns (Republicans swept the field), and it had short items on all of the deaths and weddings. It had no sports page but occasionally published reports on games played by the Normal School teams.

It also favored its readers with glimpses into the personal lives of their neighbors. It had long columns of "Brevities" and "Your Name in Print." I count eighty-nine such items in a November 1914 issue. These items were submitted by the subjects themselves or their neighbors or family. Moreover, the *Republic* had correspondents in various neighborhoods in its circulation area who reported on the doings around them and got paid by the column inch for their submissions. In that same issue, I count eleven such articles.

To give you some idea of what they learned about their neighbors, here is a sample: "The Silver Circle will meet next Monday at the home of Mrs. K.C.

Cornwell"; "Mrs. C.H. Peck of Spencerport was a Saturday guest at the home of Mrs. D.G. Crippen"; "Mrs. Rapalea has been spending the past week with her sister, Mrs. E. Mock in Macedon"; "Miss Esther Hope entertained her Sunday school class of the Baptist Church on Saturday afternoon"; "Mr. and Mrs. Clyde Amidon are rejoicing over the arrival of a young son in their home, Friday, Nov. 6th"; "Mrs. M.G. Maloney underwent an operation on Monday at the Park Avenue Hospital, Rochester"; "The Grand Central Yellows defeated the Brockport team on the Brockport Alleys Tuesday evening"; and "The condition of Glenn Holliday is reported to be much improved and he can sit up a short time each day."

The Brockport housewife was also able to plan her grocery and clothing shopping by perusing the advertisements in the Republic. Some examples of the prices that were advertised: "Canned peaches 12c"; "Canned pineapple 12c"; "Ginger snaps, per lb. 7c"; "Table syrup, 3 cans 25c"; "4 rolls toilet paper 25c"; "Corn flakes, pkg. 5c"; "Canned tomatoes, 3 cans 25c"; "6 bars Fels-Naptha soap 25c"; "Men's work socks 6c"; "Ladies dresses 49c"; "Corsets 39c"; "Men's shoes 50c–1.15"; and "Ladies' skirts 20c."

Farmers could learn about local commodity prices, as compared to those in a recent issue of the New York Times: "Corn, bu. Then 85c now 3.77" and "Wheat bu. Then 1.00 now 5.48."

Finally, F. W. Newman urged the readers to "Get a Christmas present for the Whole Family" a Ford Runabout for $440, a Ford touring car for $490, or a Ford sedan for $975.

Newspapers

The history of newspapers published in Brockport runs from 1827, when the *Brockport Free Press* began publication, until 2006, when the *Brockport Post* ceased.

The *Brockport Free Press* was part of the political organization formed by Martin Van Buren to support the presidential election campaign of Andrew Jackson. It was founded by Abiathar Harris and Thomas H. Hyatt, but Harris soon left to start an anti-Jackson newspaper. He returned in 1830 to merge the two, but left definitively in 1831 and Hyatt continued alone for another two years.

At least seventeen other newspapers were published in Brockport in the twenty-three years between the demise of the *Brockport Free Press* and the birth of the *Brockport Republic* and two others since then. Most of them published only a few issues before expiring. The longest-lived of them seems to have been the *Brockport Watchman*, which began publication in 1844 to support the Whig political party and survived until at least 1851. In 1852, it was replaced by the *Brockport Weekly Journal*, another Whig newspaper, which was short lived.

Other newspapers during that period included the *Brockport Recorder* (1828), the *Brockport Republican* (1833), the *Jeffersonian* (1835) in Clarkson, the *Brockport Sentinel* (1843), the *Brockport Weekly Journal* (1852), the *Brockport Gazette* (1858), the *Brockport Daily Advertiser* (1859).

Horatio N. Beach, the founding publisher of the *Brockport Republic*, came to Brockport from Connecticut, apparently with the intention of publishing a Republican newspaper, though he is also identified as a storekeeper. Beach became a leading businessman and politician from the late 1850s until his death in 1896 when he was succeeded as publisher by his son, Lorenzo.

The first issue of the *Republic* appeared in October 1856, just in time to support the election campaign of the first Republican presidential candidate, John C. Fremont. In July 1870, William and Charles H. Brink founded the *Brockport Democrat*, as a partisan counterpoise to the *Republic*. The two newspapers competed for fifty-five years until merging in 1925 as the *Brockport Republic-Democrat*. In reality, the *Republic* absorbed the *Democrat*.

So far as I have been able to learn, no other newspaper was published in Brockport after 1870, except that the *Temperance Times* was published weekly by the Women's Christian Temperance Union for some time after 1875 and a short-lived weekly, the *Brockport News* appeared in 1935–36.

The *Republic-Democrat* was published under a succession of owners until Kenneth Hovey closed up shop and retired in 1972. When Andrew Wolf of Pittsford, publisher of a number of small-town weeklies, learned of this, he acquired Hovey's subscription list and founded the *Brockport Post* as successor to the *Republic-Democrat*. He published the *Post* for thirty-four years, closing it down in 2006. Since then, no newspaper has been published in Brockport, the long history of Brockport newspapers came to an end. However, the *Suburban News*, published in Spencerport, covers Brockport news.

Fortunately for local historians, a nearly complete file of the *Brockport Republic* and the *Republic-Democrat* exists, in bound paper copies at the Emily L. Knapp Museum, on microfilm at several area libraries, and online and searchable at nyshistoricnewspapers.org. Except for two years from October 1864 to October 1866, there are only a few small gaps.

On the other hand, only a few, scattered copies of the *Brockport Democrat* were known to exist until a few years ago when Pete Apicela, proprietor of Java Junction, discovered thousands of copies in his third floor, which had been the print shop of the *Democrat* around the turn into the twentieth century. I sorted them out and arranged for the microfilming of about 700 of the best preserved issues. Those microfilms are available in eight area libraries.

6

Early Brockport Hotels

The late 1850s and early 1860s were a prosperous time for Brockport. Canal traffic was near its peak and Brockport had the great advantage of being a "clearing point" for canal vessels. This meant that all boats had to stop in Brockport, pay a toll, and get cleared by the Brockport toll collector. Because of that heavy lay-over traffic, Brockport's hotel business thrived. In 1862, according to an article by James Cornes in the *Brockport Democrat*, the village had five hotels.

Among the hotels were two on the north bank of the canal: the Eastern Hotel on the east side of the Main Street bridge and the Western Hotel on the west side. The largest hotel in the village was the American Hotel on the south bank on the west side of Main Street. The north bank hotels disappeared long ago, but half of the American (renamed the Landmark) was demolished to make way for the post office in 1940 and the other half was destroyed by fire in 1955.

Also downtown in 1862 was the Farmers Hotel. About the same time, Elias B. Holmes owned a hotel on the northwest corner of the Main and Erie Streets intersection where the Methodist Church is now located across the street from his residence on the southwest corner of that intersection.

Two other hotels were near the railroad depot after the New York Central arrived in 1852. The Porter Hotel was south of the tracks at the corner of Park Avenue and Fair Street. It was built in 1851 in anticipation of the arrival of the railroad and was reputed to be a favorite for lodging by farmers coming to Brockport from the south. That structure is the only building that housed a hotel still surviving in the village. For at least sixty years, it was a private residence. It is now being converted by Kevin McCarthy into a bed and breakfast. So, once again, after a long hiatus, it will be providing accommodations for travelers. In 1862, the Railroad Hotel was just west of Park Avenue's New York Central depot; it had the distinction of including a bowling alley.

Later hotels near the depot were the Lark Inn of John Larkin, prominent Brockport businessman and political leader, and the Geibel Hotel. They were on Railroad Avenue, a street along the north side of the railroad right of way that survives now as an overgrown footpath.

The heyday of hotels in Brockport is long past. There has been none since the landmark burned, though the Victorian bed and breakfast continues to offer lodgings for visitors of the village.

7

Brockport in the Great Depression

Though the stock market crash that precipitated the Great Depression occurred on October 24–29, 1929, the *Brockport Republic-Democrat* took no notice of any problems until its November 14 edition. Even then, it was only to note that the federal government had "stepped into the grain marketing situation to aid farmers" with no local reference.

The *Republic-Democrat* first called attention to local problems on December 12. It reported that the "Brockport Cheer Club" that had been organized two years earlier was "aiding the worthy poor" of whom there were estimated to be "at least two hundred people in and around Brockport ... in need of food, clothing, and coal."

In June 1930, the *Republic-Democrat* reported that "business in Brockport had been very slow," and in October, it noted that potatoes that had been worth $1.15 a bushel the previous year were now worth only 80 cents. In November, it appealed to its reader not "to hoard money," it was needed by the local merchants. That same month, rates for electricity were cut and the *BR-D* offered free work wanted classified ads for the "many who are out of work."

By December 1930, the *BR-D* headline screamed "Unemployment Causing Severe Suffering Here," and between then and March 1931, the community lost its hospital because of the "neglect or inabilities of its patrons to pay their accounts," the Brockport Agricultural Fair dissolved due to its troubled finances, and the inter-city trolley stopped running for the same reason. The hospital reopened in August 1932. In January 1931, the village board reported being plagued by unpaid taxes and cut the property tax rate from $8.30 to $7.03.

As the crisis deepened, the community rallied around to muster its means to "help the worthy poor." More than thirty persons representing twenty-four organizations met in early December 1930 as the Community Cheer Club, which had actually begun in 1928. Under the chairmanship of Mayor Shafer, they organized their efforts. They raised enough money and in-kind donations "to see that no one would be in want in this section" on Christmas Day. They distributed baskets containing "chicken, celery, evaporated milk, peas, beans, relish, tomato soup, cherries, tomatoes, macaroni, bread, jam, jelly, rice, prunes, coffee, tea, oats, flour, butter, sugar, apples, potatoes and carrots." Each December, the Cheer Club was in business again, because each year "many families ... need warm clothing, food, and toys."

The success of the private efforts to assist the needy was seen in the relatively small amount expended by the Town of Sweden for relief efforts in 1930. The *BR-D* complimented "the people of Brockport, who distributed" clothing and shoes, "saving the town a large amount of money." Those private efforts also led to the creation of vegetable gardens where those in need could raise some of their own food and a "Clothing Bureau."

As another community effort, a local committee was formed in November 1931 to participate in a county-wide "Civic Committee on Unemployment" that was conducting an "emergency employment campaign that in scope, purpose, and the solidarity of its support is believed to be without precedent in the annals of American community enterprise." A "county organization of 1,181 workers" was approaching "every resident of Monroe County" asking them "to pledge what he or she can afford to spend in the next few months for merchandise, real estate repairs, improvements in home or business property without delay." This was intended "to provide employment directly by furnishing jobs and indirectly by exercising normal purchasing power." By December 17, "10,771 individuals, firms and groups" had pledged to spend $6,026,351, but Brockporter Gifford Morgan, chairman of the western section, reported only "about $5,500."

In December 1931, Brockport suffered another financial blow when the State Bank of Commerce, one of the two banks in the village, was closed by the State Superintendent of Banks "Because of its non-liquid condition and depreciation in the value of its assets." Despite initial hopes that it would reopen, it was closed definitively in October 1932. In spite of the *BR-D*'s boast in December 1931 that the other bank, the First National, "stands like a rock," it did not reopen after the March 1933 Bank Holiday and was replaced eleven months later by the Brockport National Bank.

Another feature of Depression-era Brockport was the presence of "tramps." In September 1931, "Officers Hosner and Costigan went up to the so-called 'Jungles' [on the east side of the village] and rounded up twenty-two 'tramps'. Five were vagrants, having resided in Monroe County for the past 6 months. The others lived ... in Buffalo, Pennsylvania, Syracuse, New York City and Utica." They were arraigned in the Town Court. Twenty "were ordered to get out of town." One was released to take a job he had been promised and one was a member of the American Legion and was released because he was a World War I veteran.

In February 1933, Brockport began to benefit from "make work" projects as "around one hundred men from this town" were employed "in the County Relief Work" and twenty-eight of its boys joined the Reforestation Army. In May 1935, the Civilian Conservation Corps camp was established at Hamlin Beach State Park. Additionally, the Works Project Administration provided a subsidy for improvements of Brockport streets and the Public Works Administration allocated $495,000 for construction of the new Normal School building.

The Depression continued through 1938, but most of the impact and most of the community's responses after 1935 were pretty much the same as what had gone on before. Brockport continued to suffer and to deal with its suffering in much the same ways. The effects of the Depression and our responses to it probably mirrored those of most small towns across the country.

8

Entertainment and Events

Movies

The forerunner of the movie theater was the nickelodeon, usually a small theater, sometimes seating as many as 200 viewers, but often only twenty or thirty. They charged 5 cents for admission and projected short films, sometimes no more than a few minutes long. They flourished from 1905 until about 1913. By 1908, the U.S. had more than 8,000 nickelodeons.

Beginning about 1907, longer, feature-type films were being produced and theaters became larger. In that year, suddenly three such movie theaters appeared in Brockport, the Dream Works on King Street, Dreamland, (location unknown), and the Bijou Dream in the Opera House Block, a three-story building on the site of Bicycle Outfitters. In 1908, they were joined by the Happy Hour (location unknown) and the Lyric on the ground floor of the north half of the Winslow Building, which is now the Strand, and in 1909 by the Hippodrome in the American Hotel building where the post office is now. How long the Dream Works and Dreamland survived is not known, but, probably, by 1909, Brockport had six movie theaters, but at least four.

In 1914, the Globe opened at 69 Main Street and Brockport acquired an open air movie theater, the Airdome, on a parking lot at Erie and Queen Streets. It claimed to have seating for 700–800 viewers.

In 1912, apparently responding to criticism, the Lyric ran a notice claiming that its music was the "very latest and best to be had" with an $800 Witney player piano. (Witneys were manufactured in Brockport.) Its "pickture machine" was new and its "projecting lenses" had been custom made. The films were projected onto a

10 × 14-foot "solid wall." The building was "well-ventilated and fireproof" and it showed "no vulgar or indecent subjects."

The movies shown were usually short documentaries. *Roosevelt in Africa*, war films, prison life, auto manufacturing, raising the battleship *Maine*, the James boys, the coronation of King George, the Mexican War, the passion play at Oberammergau were some that played in Brockport theaters. Also, they ran serials, sometimes going twenty or thirty episodes. They showed cartoons, travel pictures, newsreels, and commercial documentaries (the Larkin Soap Co., for instance). Fictional dramas began in 1915 with D. W. Griffith's two-hour-long epic, *Birth of a Nation*.

Brockport's early movie theaters were venues for other events as well. They presented plays, variety shows, magic shows, singers, operas, beauty contests, vaudeville acts, fashion shows, minstrels, and elocutionists. They sponsored contests and had drawings for prizes. As late as the 1940s, movie theaters had drawings for sets of china or $5 bags of groceries on Saturday evenings.

In 1908, the Strand opened on the second floor of the Winslow Building. The Lyric continued on the ground floor for a short time, but the Strand really became its successor. The Globe disappeared about the same time. Brockport remained a one movie theater town, except for a few years in the 1980s, when the Studio operated on King Street. The talkies came to the Strand in 1929. The Strand is one of only two movie theaters to have survived among the thousands that started in those heady days of the movie craze between 1907 and 1910. It was exceeded in age only by the Newtown Theater in Newtown, Pennsylvania that opened in 1906.

Old Home Week

The greatest celebration in the history of Brockport was the Old Home Week on Fourth of July week in 1911. It featured different themes each day and attracted many visitors and former residents despite the "intense" heat, reaching 95 to 100 degrees. Special editions of a newspaper, an elaborate brochure, and special postcards were published. The public was invited to contribute toward the costs. The *Brockport Republic* printed a list of donors already on May 18th that included eighty-nine names with donations ranging from 25 cents to $50.

It began on Monday, July 3, as Normal School Day and Children's Day. Anyone who had ever attended the Normal School was invited back. Children from the Grammar School and the parochial schools participated also. The Fourth of July festivities were the high point of the week. They included an oration by a celebrated speaker from Watertown, a parade of floats led by the National Guard, a "vaudeville show," and fireworks. All of the downtown buildings were decorated with flags and bunting. The *Republic* reported attendance of "at least 10,000."

Wednesday was Athletic Day, featuring track and field competitions and a baseball game between the Normal team and a visiting nine. Thursday was firemen's day with a parade of firefighting vehicles and bands from neighboring companies as well as the Brockporters. Also, there was a "prize contest," races, and drills. Friday was fraternal day. A parade of the members of lodges, societies, church organizations, and Sunday school classes was scheduled, but "no fraternities appeared … owing to the intense heat." Still, there were band concerts and vaudeville acts. Saturday was Rochester Day with "speeches, a parade, and exercises" intended to open Brockport's doors "to our neighbors from the city." For Sunday, the churches were asked to "prepare special exercises and music to greet any former members."

The Brockport Concert Band was enlisted to provide music all week, with a program of sacred music on Sunday. Thirty-eight decorated arches lining downtown streets were illuminated by 3,000 red and yellow electric lights, giving "Brockport the appearance of an enchanted land." Main Street was "filled with booths, a merry-go-round, vaudeville stages, etc., and a midway."

The *Republic* published a "Partial List of Those Who Registered at Official Booth," which contained ninety-nine names. Most came from towns in western New York, but one came from Pasadena, Calif., six from Michigan, two from Des Moines, three from Chicago, and a scattering from Massachusetts, New Jersey, Ohio, New Hampshire, and Washington, D.C. In addition, the *Republic* published personal notices about still other visitors.

Despite the "intense" heat, everyone seems to have had a good time, but, apparently, not good enough to repeat it. At least, more than a century has passed without another Old Home Week.

Fourth of July in the 1860s

Fourth of July usually began at midnight of July 3rd and ended in the early hours of the morning of July 5th. Great preparations would be made by the village's men and boys. The older men laid out the program for the general exercises of the day, including the reading of the Declaration of Independence and Washington's Farewell Address, speechmaking, singing, and a display of fireworks.

The young men made preparations to have a good time by the ringing of bells, firing of cannons, clanging of anvils, drumming of the bass drums, and making a most hideous noise on what was called a horse fiddle, which was made by stretching across the top of a small barrel two or three strips of horse hide, making a bow of the same material, and knocking out a hole in the bottom of the barrel. Then the material with which to build the bonfire was looked after. Everybody contributed in order to make the windup of the day's celebration a success.

Besides the instruments, some boys would gain entrance to the belfries of the churches, attach a cord to the bell, drop the same to someone waiting, who would take it to the opposite side of the street. At midnight on the Fourth, the booming of a cannon would begin the fun. Pandemonium broke loose, bells rang, cannons boomed, all the other instruments going, groups paraded with the horse fiddle up and down the street, the bonfire started, boys and girls and young men came from all directions with boxes, barrels, cord wood, and anything that would burn.

The younger boys would make all the noise possible with small cannons, shotguns, and everything that would add to the pandemonium. Almost all the people in the village would be awakened and were cross enough to want to lick someone, and at the same time knew that it was no use to "frumble" or find fault as there was no remedy until the sport was ended about 3 or 4 a.m.

At daylight on the Fourth, the program of the day would take place and then the night of the Fourth would be a repetition of the previous night except that at almost every house in the village in the early part of the evening would be a display of fireworks consisting of firecrackers, pinwheels, Roman candles, skyrockets, etc., until the time came for an elaborate display by the citizens committee, usually from a platform at the corner of Main and Market Streets.

Besides the usual display of rockets, Roman candles, red lights, etc., there would be elaborate pieces illustrating the signing of the Declaration of Independence, Washington crossing the Delaware, and many others. The display would begin about 9 or 9.30 p.m. and would last until midnight. Then would come the big bonfire, which wound everything up. Everyone joined in the fun and had a good time. Such a fire would light up the whole village and could be seen for miles. From the surrounding country, it would look as if the whole village was burning up.

Hallowe'en

This essay will look at how Hallowe'en was celebrated in some past years. First, what happened a century ago? The *Brockport Republic* dropped some hints that there had been some Hallowe'en vandalism in earlier years, but I could not find any reports to confirm that. Nevertheless, on October 29, 1914, it warned: "Boys should be careful not to carry their Hallowe'en pranks so far that they become practical jokes. A strict watch will be kept for malicious mischief makers." Also, the *Republic* referred to "some of the depredations in times past." In fact, those mischief makers might have been discouraged in other years as well, for it was usually reported that Hallowe'en witnessed an increased police presence.

In fact, Hallowe'en in 1914 seems to have been celebrated almost entirely with private parties. "A crowd of Brockport young men" gave a Hallowe'en party in Singleton Hall. Fagan's orchestra furnished the music and dinner was served. Mrs.

L. B. Shafer and Mrs. James Mann acted as chaperones for the thirty couples who attended. At the Normal School, "Arethusa entertained the new Normal students and the faculty at a Hallowe'en Party. The program was as follows: Song, Miss Cummings; Piano Solo, Miss Dean; Vocal Solo, Miss Spicer, Ghost Story, Miss Claire Williams; Ghost Dance, Miss Leonard (leader), Miss Whipple, Miss Andross and Miss Lee. Games, dancing and refreshments followed the program."

Things were quite different in the 1930s. Beginning in 1930, the Kiwanis Club sponsored Hallowe'en parades and parties centered on the Public Building, where the Market Street fire hall is now. Paul Hanks, Sr., seems to have been the main organizer. Their purpose, the Kiwanians announced, was "to provide wholesome amusements and a cessation of the rowdyism which has resulted in damage to property." The celebrations consisted of a parade, "sports," games, stunts, costumes, and prizes. Music was provided by the Brockport Fife and Drum Corps or the high school band. The 1933 parade was described by the *Republic* as "huge" and included torch lights. The economic Depression that was afflicting the country at that time seems to have been very much on the partiers' minds. In 1931, the parade included a white hearse drawn by two white horses and bearing a large sign saying "We are bearing the Depression," and in 1933, a float depicted "old man Depression."

The 1936 celebration was the last. In 1937, it was announced that there would be no parade because it was a Saturday and the streets would be crowded with shoppers. The "police believe they will have all they can handle in taking care of the usual Saturday night traffic without adding a parade of youngsters dodging around cars, etc. The risk and responsibility will be too much for the Club to assume." The village board added an announcement that "as early as October 19," windows on businesses had been soaped, and so had the sign at the Seymour Library and part of a stone fence had been removed. Also, the village trustees sternly lectured, "Children, listen, you never had a library outside of the school until the Seymour Library was established and the Library Board has spent a great deal of money in filling up a special room for you and in buying books for your enjoyment. Surely you want to do your part. Damage to the library costs money and if the Board has to spend some for this reason, the benefits you receive there will be lessened."

The Brockport Fair

From 1857 until 1933, with gaps in 1870–76 and 1932, the biggest event of the year was Brockport's agricultural fair. It began in 1857 as the Brockport Union Agricultural Society's rival to the county fair that its founders believed was too far away to be convenient for exhibitors from the western towns in Monroe County and the eastern towns in Orleans County. It was called the Brockport Union Agricultural Fair.

The towns were Murray, Clarendon, and Kendall in Orleans County and Sweden, Clarkson, Union (later named Hamlin), Parma, and Ogden in Monroe County. Elias B. Holmes, Brockport's wealthiest resident, farm owner, and horse breeder, was the founding president. Horatio N. Beach, publisher of the *Republic*, was secretary and Thomas Cornes was treasurer. Each of the towns appointed two vice-presidents.

The first fair was held in October 1857 with 810 entries and $305 in premiums. To help finance the project, 191 ten-year memberships were sold for $10 apiece. So, apparently, it was widely perceived as a valuable civic endeavor. For several years in the early 1860s, a floral and horse show was added. The 1860 June show featured eighteen floral exhibitors and 111 horses. By 1861, fifty-nine sheep, butter, and farm implements were added. The October fair in 1861 was sufficiently popular that a special train brought attendees from Rochester.

Typically, entries in the October 1863 fair included eighty-two cattle, 108 horses, 188 sheep, one swine, eleven poultry, forty-three ladies manufacture, eleven mechanical, thirty-three general manufacture, seven fine arts, 100 agricultural products, fourteen butter and cheese, seven floral, eighteen bread, wine, etc., and eight miscellaneous. Entertainment was added with the Clarendon Cornet Band performing.

In 1863, Frederick P. Root replaced Holmes and George B. Whiteside became treasurer. Although the 1867 fair was deemed the most successful yet, the event was discontinued after the 1869 running. It resumed in 1877 with a lineup of exhibitors very similar to those of the 1860s. Horse races were added.

The fair grew considerably by 1899, when its disbursements amounted to $5,305.17 and it "stands first in the state in amount of premiums paid." Also, it undertook substantial improvements to the buildings on the fairgrounds and bought more land.

In later years, the fair added entertainment features, band music, ball games, boys' foot races, and bicycle races. In 1900, for instance, it booked one-legged bicyclists, acrobats and comedians, and aerialists. That year, also, the promoters took note of the demise of their rival county fair and claimed a record number of entries.

In February 1901, the society voted to sponsor the county fair, terminated its connection with Orleans County towns, and changed its name to Monroe County Agricultural Society. For the next thirty years, the fair grew and became more elaborate. By 1930, it had added a carnival with several rides and twenty "shows" that employed 500 and traveled in a special train of thirty cars. Also, it now featured a fife and drum corps, a band concert, balloon ascensions, parachute exhibitions, fireworks, educational features, a firemen's parade, sports, and other contests. That year, the society voted to build a grandstand.

Despite such seeming success, the Brockport fair's days were numbered. In 1931, the fair was cancelled because it failed to receive the state subsidy that had financed the prizes. Rochester took advantage of that cancellation to usurp the Monroe County Fair and add it as a supplement to its Rochester Exposition.

Brockport returned in 1932 for a swansong. In desperate moves to survive, the admission price was reduced to 25 cents and the dates were pushed back to September. The *Republic* added, hopefully, that a special attraction might be "that some local couple will be secured to take the marriage vows the first evening." But it also warned ominously that if "the attendance at the fair does not show support of the people, then the Brockport exhibition may be classed as done for."

Apparently, the necessary support was not forthcoming, though Brockport received a $4,794 subsidy from the state. The 1933 fair was the last. In January 1934, the society voted to dissolve and sell the fairgrounds to the village for $2,200. Brockport's voters opted to accept the offer by an eighty-vote margin in a 1,000-vote turnout. So ended Brockport's long run as host to an agricultural fair.

Brockport Town Baseball Teams

Brockport has a long history of what were called "town baseball teams." The first reference that I could find in the *Brockport Republic* to a local "base-ball" team was June 13 and 20, 1867, when the Brockport Eclipse beat the Albion Amateur, 72–54. Judging by the score, "base-ball" must have been a bit different from today's baseball. By 1870, the Brockport team was called the Korekt and lost to Cortland Normal, 56–24. In 1872, a "Brockport Base Ball Club" was organized with "Regulations and by-laws" and a set of officers. However, the *BR* reported six weeks later that it had been "short-lived."

Skipping the interim and fast forwarding to June 1926, a "Brockport Twilight Baseball League" was organized with, guess-who as president—the original Nat O. Lester. Four teams formed the league: the A&P Products Corp., Moore-Shafer Co., Business men, and "the scholastic nine." As many as 2,000 fans attended the twice-weekly games. In 1927, the Brockporters joined the D. & C. League, which included teams from Albion, Holley, Caledonia, Scottsville, Hilton, Charlotte, and Irondequoit. Brockport was to draw its players from Sweden, Clarkson, and Hamlin, including the best of the Twilight League.

The golden age of Brockport town teams arrived when Edwin E. Nihiser joined the Normal School faculty as head of the physical education and manual training department in 1928. Also, he coached the basketball and baseball teams. He was from Hagerstown, Md., and had graduated from the University of Maryland and taught manual training and coached athletics at the Mountain Park Institute in North Carolina. He had also played professional baseball with the Baltimore Orioles and Reading, Pa., of the International League.

In 1929, with Nihiser as coach-pitcher, the Brockport team, now called the Freezers, were the champions in the Western Division of the D. and C. League with a 9–1 record. Nihiser pitched a no hit 9–0 victory and hit a homerun to win the division championship. Meanwhile, Nihiser's baseball and basketball teams were the 1929 N.Y.S. Normal School champions.

The Freezers finished the 1930 season out of the running, but bounced back in 1931 to win the State Rural Baseball championship with a 20–0 season. They scored 190 runs to sixty-one for their opponents. Nihiser was replaced as manager for the 1932 season but remained on the team as a pitcher. That year, the Freezers had a 13–0 season and were the Western New York champions. On September 29, the team's thirty-eight-game win streak ended—and so did Brockport's golden age.

The Freezers were replaced by the Brockport Athletics in 1932 and the Brockport Merchants in 1934. Both teams had mediocre records. An attempt was made to resurrect the Freezers in 1938 as a team in the Orleans County Baseball League, but nothing came of it. Nihiser was on sabbatical from the Normal School in 1934–35 and returned as director of health education for men. He resumed his role as coach and, in 1947, was head of the department of industrial arts, but town teams participating in inter-town leagues never returned.

Indian Visits

This essay quotes an article in the *Brockport Democrat* of about 1900. It was part of a series of reminiscences by Brockporter James Cornes. They were transcribed by Harold Dobson and A. B. Elwell. Sue Savard came upon their transcription and Charlie Cowling, the college archivist, posted it. Here is an excerpt from it, with a bit of editing:

> The Preston place [on the east side of Brockport] was the camping place for the Indians who visited annually. In front of the Preston place was a grove in which the Indians would camp and proceed to make baskets, willow mats, etc. The first intimation the inhabitants would know of their arrival would be the appearance of the Indian squaws on the streets, vending their wares, and the appearance of the young and old bucks with their bows and arrows ready to show their skill. Then almost everybody on the streets would be seen sticking up the old fashioned copper cent on a stick or the cork of a bottle for the Indian boys to shoot at, the copper to belong to the one who first hit it with his arrow. I have seen seven or eight Indian boys and men at a time along Main Street shooting at copper cents. Sometimes, someone would put up a silver dime. Then you would see a half dozen braves, all eager to get the first shot, for the one who struck the coin claimed it, but if he struck the stick or bottle and thus jarred the coin off, it was replaced and the next one took a shot.
>
> I have seen the squaws come in to Brockport carrying on their heads and backs a load of baskets, from six quarts to one-half bushel in size, which would puzzle an ordinary drayman to load onto a one-horse cart.

> Upon the advent of the Indians becoming noised about, half the inhabitants of the village would be down to the encampment watching them ply their avocation of basket making and all the features of Indian life.
>
> Then would usually come the Indian show, generally given in the old village hall. At the shows would usually be given an illustration of Indian warfare, trials of marksmanship with bow and arrow, the Indian war dance, the big medicine man driving out the evil spirit from the sick woman, etc. These people would be dressed in all the glory of the primitive Indian—buffalo and bear skins and bear and buffalo heads for disguises. Then the regular Indian tom-toms, their war whoops, throwing knives and tomahawks, imitation of scalping, etc., are all remembered by the older inhabitants.

The last performance of this kind given by genuine Indians was about the year of 1866 or shortly after the Civil War.

Pigeons

This essay is an excerpt from James Cornes's reminiscences as published in the *Brockport Democrat*:

> In the early 1850s, squirrels, red, gray, and black were in abundance in the woods east of the village, also partridges and quail, wood cock and snipe abounded almost everywhere, and passenger pigeons flew so thick that it was nothing to think of getting 10 or 20, or more than one could carry in two or three hours of time of hunting. At almost any time of the year and in early Spring when the pigeons were returning from their annual flight to the south, it was no unusual thing for hunters to shoot two or three hundred a day. I have seen them fly so thick in almost continuous flocks, both Spring and Fall, that they would almost darken the sun. I have seen from 20 to 50 men and boys with guns stationed some in the eastern part of town, some in the south and west and, in fact everywhere in and out of the corporation all shooting pigeons. The flight spoken of would sometimes last for eight or ten days, and for a month or two after, pigeons would fly in their ordinary flights which would mean 25 or 30 flocks a day containing from a hundred or more birds, to a flock consisting of thousands, and such flights were ordinary and caused no comment. I remember one Spring when birds flew so thick that the late Charles Van Eps stood opposite my father's house on South St. and in front of D.S. Morgan's barn and before 10 o'clock in the morning had so many pigeons that he could not carry them all home.

As late as 1870, the *Brockport Republic* could report:

> For two or three weeks large flocks of wild pigeons have been flying northward. A party of four or five went down to the lakeshore the forepart of the week and in a few hours shot over two hundred. The pigeons fly low and those killed were shot as the flocks were flying along the fields near the lake. We hear that there are many pigeons in the woods in all directions.

It also could report that "A great many wild pigeons have been shot in this locality recently. It is believed that they come from Pennsylvania, where they had a 'roost' during the summer." These accounts suggest that Brockporters played a role in the extermination of the passenger pigeons that once numbered in the billions. The last survivor died in the Cincinnati zoo in 1910.

9

Higher Education

The Village and the College

It has been said that, "If it weren't for the college, Brockport would be just another Holley." Leaving aside the implied insult toward our neighboring village, that opinion is patently false. Much more accurate would be, "If it weren't for the village, the college would not exist."

The college celebrated its 175th anniversary in 2010, making official a founding date of its earliest antecedent as 1835. This was based on the fact that a building for a Baptist college was nearly completed in that year and a principal was appointed. However, there is no evidence that any students were enrolled or any classes conducted. We do know that the building was sold in foreclosure in 1836, so the school appears to have become defunct within a year. Now, recently, a document has come to light that seems to show conclusively that the Baptist college never functioned.

The document, dated February 1, 1837, reports that a Provisional Charter for the college had been granted that would become "operative" if supporters of the college raised $80,000 within three years of its issuance. The document lists pledges to that date of $1,750—far short of the amount required. As the three years seem to have expired, the conditions of the charter had not been met and the college could not have come into existence. The building was later acquired for the Brockport Collegiate Institute, which began in 1841 and is the earliest verifiable antecedent of today's College at Brockport.

The origins of the college lie in a meeting of village leaders in 1830 that invited the Western New York Baptist Conference to designate Brockport the site of the college it was planning. The Baptists accepted that invitation in late 1830. A village leader donated 6 acres of land and $3,000 to build a building for the proposed college. Though the college never came into being, the building survived.

In 1841, village leaders founded the Brockport Collegiate Institute in the abandoned building. In 1854, the building burned. Once again, village residents came to the rescue, raised the necessary funds, and paid for a new building. Ten years later, the institution was floundering financially, and, in 1866, the village board covered the school's debts through taxation and successfully petitioned the State to site one of the new "normal schools" in Brockport.

The Normal School ran into severe difficulties in the depression years of the 1930s with low enrollment and a badly deteriorating physical plant. The State considered closing the institution or using it to house a correctional facility for women. Once again, the village rallied to its support, formed a "Committee of One Hundred" to campaign for its survival, and sent a delegation to meet with Vincent Dailey, a Brockport native and son of a prominent Brockport businessman. He was political secretary to Governor Lehman.

Dailey intervened to save the school as a "State Teachers College." He told the delegation that they could keep the college, but the existing buildings would be demolished and replaced by one built on the blueprints of one recently completed in Plattsburgh. He picked up a phone, called the state budget director, and told him to include funds for that purpose in the 1938 budget. So, for the fifth time, the village saved the college.

Throughout its first century, the college never enrolled more than a few hundred students, mostly residents of the Brockport area and was almost always shaky financially. Brockport's manufacturing industries had a much greater impact on the life, growth, and character of the village than did the college.

At one time, Brockport was a major farm machinery production center. At least six factories produced farm implements, including the largest industrial plant in Monroe County. Over the years, Brockport manufactured many other products and had at least nine food processing plants. After World War II, General Electric employed 1,400 workers and Owens-Illinois had 700. Until GE, Owens-Illinois, and A&P closed in the mid-1980s, manufacturing was much the largest employer in the village. Perhaps, without manufacturing, Brockport would be just another Holley.

In recent years, the college has become the greatest influence, both good and bad, on the village. It brings great benefits, in culture, in volunteerism, in vitality for our downtown, but it also brings deterioration of our housing stock, some disorder, and a drain on the village budget.

Brockport Collegiate Institute in 1847

The Brockport Collegiate Institute in 1847 was housed in a four-story stone structure, 60 × 100 feet. One wing on the first floor included Mrs. Bates's dwelling and boarding spaces, rooms for teachers, and study rooms for young ladies. The other wing contained recitation and study rooms for young gentlemen. Upstairs were four general school rooms, a chapel, and thirty-two study rooms. Each study room had a bedroom attached and rented for $2 per room per student. Students paid $112 for tuition, board, room, bed and bedding, towels, washing, mending, wood, and lights. Enrollment for 1847–48 included 239 males and 156 females.

The extent to which dormitory life has changed over the years (or not?) may be seen by comparing the set of rules for students at the Brockport Collegiate Institute for 1847 with today's situation.

RULES

Article I: No student may make alteration in his or her room without permission from the principal.
Article II: All damages done to any room shall be immediately repaired at the occupant's expense.
Article III: All damages where the culprit is not known, shall be charged in a bill of common damages paid equally by those occupying the apartment.
Article IV: The Prudential Committee shall visit all rooms twice each term to assess damages.
Article V: Every student shall attend church on Sunday unless specially excused.
Article VI: No student may keep or use firearms or gunpowder in or about the building.
Article VII: Young ladies may not receive calls from young gentlemen in their rooms.
Article VIII: No student will be allowed to play cards or other games of chance or hazard.
Article IX: No student may use a stove pipe larger than 6 inches.
Article X: Each student must have a pail of water in his room at the time of retiring.
Article XI: No student may keep matches in his room unless they are placed safely in a tin box.
Article XII: No wood may be kept in the room except in wood boxes.
Article XIII: No student may throw water or ashes or any other thing out the window.
Article XIV: No student may visit taverns, grocery stores or any public place for the purpose of entertainment or pleasure.
Article XV: No student may use intoxicating drinks or tobacco in any form in this institute or on the grounds, nor employ immodest or profane language of any description.

Despite Articles X and XI, the building burned to the ground in 1854.

The Brockport Collegiate Institute in 1859

James Balfour had just become an instructor in foreign languages at the Brockport Collegiate Institute in 1859. He wrote two letters to a former colleague with whom he had taught at a school in Marietta, Ohio. This was five years after the school had suffered a disastrous fire and eight years before it morphed into the State Normal School. He wrote, in part:

> As much as I have seen of the establishment I like it very well indeed. Everything is arranged according to time, and the greatest order and quietness is maintained.... I have got a nice little room 10 feet high with a closet attached to it. The window is towards the west and about 20 rods from the house is the railroad. Sitting at my writing table I can see the cars passing by 10 times a day five trains east and five west. Especially nights it looks pretty to see them flitting by as if they were wandering stars.... Yesterday afternoon I began my first lessons in French and German. The class in the former language in the Institute will only consist of 5 or 6 at first, in the German of 4 to 5....
>
> The order of the house is: At half past six the bell is rung for all to get up, at 7 o'clock the breakfast is ready when all the teachers and the boarders sit together at one table and partake of a well prepared substantial meal. At a quarter before nine the bell is rung for chapel services, ladies and gentlemen meet together. The rolls are called a few verses in the Bible are read and a short prayer said and then school is called, the recitations last from one half hour to three quarters. At a quarter past 12 dinner is ready when we meet in the same way as in the morning. The afternoon recitations are from 1 ½ to 4 ½ o'clock supper at 5. From 7 to 9 are study hours for the students, at 9 o'clock they are called into the Principal's apartments, where after a short prayer and the singing of a hymn social intercourse is held. We have some music, conversation or a little reading, just as it suits everyone.... Yesterday afternoon we had some fine speaking and composition. The former was done by the boys, the latter read by the girls.
>
> They have given me a good deal to do, for besides the German and French, I have several Greek and Latin classes, and also a large composition and declamation class.

Such was academic life in Brockport 160 years ago. Things have changed a bit.

10

Infrastructure

Lake Road

The proprietors of the Triangular Tract of which the Town of Sweden became a part initiated the settlement effort in 1801 by contracting to have a road built to bisect the area, running from the southern tip of the property at what is now Leroy to the shore of Lake Ontario at Sandy Creek.

According to an account by one of the road builders, many years later, it took six men four days to cut a swath four rods wide the 25-mile distance following an old Indian trail. It could not have been more than the "road that a wagon could go down" required by the contract. The road was so primitive that trees had to be blazed to mark the route.

Marmion Peters, another of the workers, wrote a colorful description of the way they toiled. Here it is as reported in the *Batavia Times* in 1896:

> Its crookedness is accounted for on the ground that those laying it out had too big a stock of "tangle foot" in their supplies.
>
> The party coming to the Black Creek could not ford it, and went east to where the present Lake Road bridge crosses the creek. They were soon across the creek and worked lively until noon, when they found themselves a little south of what is now Sweden Centre. Here they crossed a small swamp by going over some logs and some little ridges like a hog's back. North of it they found a spring where they took their dinner. They took a smoke and started on working quite fast and went into camp on the ridge, which did not yet have a road.

North of the ridge the land dropped off into a dismal swamp covered with water from one to twelve inches deep. "Well, it might be called the 'black north'", Peters said. Getting firewood and eating supper occupied more than an hour and they turned in for the night about ten o'clock, "Not forgetting our bitters," said Peters, "as they were necessary, we thought, to keep the ague off; or at least that was the excuse."

The next morning they headed back south, says Peters, "well filled with fish fowl and venison, and slightly moistened with 'tangle foot', which now owing to its scarcity we were obliged to use sparingly—no taverns every mile then". As they had not marked the trees on their way north, they did so as they returned. He concludes his account, "You will see that the road from the creek to the bridge is not as crooked as south of the creek to Le Roy. The reason is that the bottles through which we took observations were nearly empty."

The Origins of Brockport Streets

The 1822 village had the streets on the west side of Main Street from the canal to Adams Street and on the east side from the canal to the intersection of Main Street and Park Avenue, then known as Mechanic Street. North of the canal were no streets on the east side and only Smith Street, then called Jones Street, and a West Street that apparently was never built. Bordering the canal on the north was Canal West Street. West College Street and Millard Street, among the original streets, were displaced by the expansion of the college after World War II.

Market Street was known as Lawrence Street and Monroe Avenue as Monroe Street. Utica Street from College Street to Adams Street was North Street, though it was one of the most southerly streets in the village. South Street is now in the middle of the village, but was then the most southerly cross street on the east side.

When the railroad arrived in 1852, Railroad Avenue was added along the north edge of the right of way. It exists now as an overgrown footpath. Sometime between 1872 and 1890, the village annexed the area south of Adams Street and laid out the streets there. Centennial Avenue was so named because it was dedicated in 1889 on the centennial of George Washington's inauguration as President. In 1964, the Havenwood, Cloverwood, Candlewick, and Meadow Lane area was annexed and the streets laid out.

Both East and West Avenues were originally called Clarkson Street. Fayette Street was named for the French marquis, apparently in commemoration of his 1824 Grand Tour of the United States. He traveled through the village on the Erie Canal. Legend says that he leaned on his cane and waved to the villagers. However, his secretary kept a diary of the trip and, according to it, their boat would have passed Brockport at 1 or 2 a.m., so the marquis was probably sleeping peacefully.

Another myth holds that some of our cross streets do not align because of hostility between Hiel Brockway and James Seymour. More likely, it was required by the "swampiness" of the area at the time. For instance, the grounds of the Morgan-Manning House were swampy, so South Street could not align with Monroe Avenue, and a swamp west of Main Street forced Clinton Street further north than Water Street.

The Village Clock

The village clock is a Seth Thomas Tower Clock. Seth Thomas was America's pre-eminent clockmaker in the period between 1813 and his death in 1859. His three sons continued the business after his death. The company went through several mergers or acquisitions, but remained in the business of manufacturing clocks until 2009, nearly two centuries after its founding. The tower clocks were produced from 1873 until 1941.

Company records show that thousands of these clocks were installed in the United States and in twenty-five foreign countries or territories. Monroe County had seventeen. Besides the village clock, F. H. Gordon had one in Brockport. Where in the village is a big question. So far as I can tell, ours is the only one in the county to have survived, though they do come up for sale occasionally. A Seth Thomas Tower Clock was offered recently in an online auction with a starting bid of $28,000.

Our clock was a project of the local chapter of the Daughters of the American Revolution, though they ran a fundraising campaign to get broader community support. They intended it as a memorial to thirty-one Revolutionary War veterans buried in the Brockport area and to early settlers in the area.

At 10:40 a.m., May 19, 1914, five D.A.R. women set it in motion to "begin its term of long service." It had taken eight days for a technician from the Seth Thomas Clock Co. to install it. Local men did the carpentry and electrical work. Half a ton of weights, one on the timing side with a fall of 10 feet 8 inches and one on the "strike" side falling 32 feet, activated the mechanism.

The dedication of the clock on June 20 was a great celebration. The D.A.R. urged residents to decorate their homes and businesses in a patriotic way and businesses to close during the ceremony. The *Republic* estimated an audience of 1,500, including many officers of the state D.A.R. and neighboring chapters. They expected the National President General, but she did not show up.

The village president, the Normal School principal, and the head of the local Sons of the American Revolution chapter spoke. A George P. Decker of Rochester, whose credentials were never reported in the *Republic*, delivered the keynote address. The Brockport Band performed and the ceremony concluded with the audience singing "America." Mrs. Fred Gordon hosted a luncheon for visiting dignitaries at her mansion in Clarkson and Mrs. George C. Gordon did the same at her home on Main Street.

The D.A.R. presented the clock to the village, which hired Guy C. Andrews to wind it weekly for $35 annual pay. Like the grandfather's clock of the song, it ran for "ninety years without slumbering," until, in 2004, "it stopped short [seemingly] never to run again." A $5,000 member's item from the state legislature paid for minor repairs and it slogged on for another eleven years. However, in 2015, it stopped again and required extensive repairs. The Brockport Lions Club, led by David Moore and Amy Gonzalez, conducted a fund drive that raised nearly $18,000 and the Rochester Area Community Foundation awarded an $11,000 grant to the village. As the repairs cost $21,500, about $6,000 was placed in a reserve fund for maintenance. Presumably, the clock will continue "its long term of service" with no more slumbering for another ninety years or so.

11

Politics

Village Elections

Brockport elections in the fifty years ending a century ago, 1866 to 1916, the period between two wars, were quite different, in many respects, from those today.

First, at the beginning of the period, the board presidents and many trustees served one-year terms, compared to four-year terms today.

Second, women got the vote in New York State only in 1917, except that women who owned property could vote on propositions to raise taxes and the *Republic* reported that eight of them did in a 1915 referendum. Also, two women were listed as voters as early as the 1865 census and women who had children or owned property could vote in school board elections from 1880.

Third, until 1894, voting was not secret. Each political party printed its own ballots and distributed them to its supporters, who deposited them in the ballot boxes. So, anyone could see which party's ballot a voter cast. The lever-operated voting machine, which permitted secrecy, had first been used in Lockport in 1892 and Brockport had adopted that method by 1894, when voters could choose between the machines and the earlier system.

Fourth, throughout the period under review, the chief executive officer of the Village was called President, rather than Mayor, and, from 1866 through 1871, was selected by the five trustees from among their number at their first, organizational, meeting. Thereafter, Presidents were chosen by the electorate.

Fifth, although as many as four tickets competed in the elections, many of the same names appeared on every ticket. Often only one or two offices were contested.

Sixth, trustees served without pay. In fact, a proposition to pay the trustees salaries totaling not more than a total of $1,000 for the five of them was defeated by a vote of 157 to forty-nine.

Seventh, there was much less stability in office. In that fifty-year period, twenty-four men held the office of president. John H. Kingsbury and George R. Ward were each elected five times, Luther Gordon and Franklin F. Capen four times each, and Thomas Cornes and George B. Harmon three times each; however, none of them served more than three consecutive terms. Therefore, no president remained in office as long as a single mayoral term today, much less Jim Stull's twenty years or the eight years of both Mary Ann Thorpe and Margay Blackman.

Trusteeships were similarly unstable. Ninety-five men occupied the four trusteeships during that period, and they served terms of varying length—two years, one year, or simply to fill a vacancy. Edgar Brown was elected nine times between 1870 and 1880 and Nelson A. Smith was elected seven times between 1877 and 1885. On the other hand, fifty men—more than half—served a single term.

Eighth, more village offices were elective throughout the period. From 1866 through 1872, they were clerk, treasurer, assessors, collector, police constable, police justice, street commissioner, and pound keeper. From 1873 through 1916, they were treasurer, collector, and assessors, except that collector was omitted in 1915 and 1916. However, many of the candidates for those offices were unopposed. For instance, John R. Davis was unopposed as treasurer from 1894 through 1916.

Finally, almost every election included voting on propositions. Many matters now handled by the board, with or without public hearings, were decided by the electorate then. Often, it seems that the board referred business to referendums simply because it had difficulty deciding them. Some examples: in 1915, a referendum approved the purchase of a motor fire truck for $1,000, but in 1916, they defeated a proposition to buy one for $2,000. Year after year, referendums considered proposals to sponsor summer band concerts, approving them in 1911 and 1913, but rejecting them in 1910, 1912, 1914, and 1916; in 1910, they refused to make the offices of village clerk and street commissioner elective, and in 1914, they refused to create a board of water commissioners.

In one important respect, however, the practice of that period has survived. Village elections were always non-partisan—that is, the tickets bore only the names of local parties, as is the case today. On the other hand, Town of Sweden elections were always partisan, Republicans and Democrats, as they are today.

The 1866 Congressional Elections

The 1866 election took place against the backdrop of the Civil War, Lincoln's assassination, and the feud between Andrew Johnson, the "accidental" Democrat in the White House, and the Congress controlled by Radical Republicans. Politics then, locally and nationally, was about as chaotic as it is now.

As an off-year election, the main contest locally concerned the Congressional seat for this district. The freshman Representative, Republican Roswell Hart, was running for re-election as a supporter of the Radical Republican Reconstruction policies. Hart was a Rochester native, a lawyer, and a businessman. He had not held public office before his election to Congress in 1864.

Hart was opposed by Lewis Selye, a former Whig turned Republican running as a "Johnsonite" independent. Selye came to Rochester from Chittenango in 1824 at the age of twenty-one. He had been trained as a blacksmith, but turned to the manufacture of iron implements and, eventually, fire engines, one of which is owned by the Capen Hose Co. While still in his thirties, he began a successful political career, serving several terms on the Monroe County Board of Supervisors and the Rochester Common Council. He was also county treasurer for several years. Thus, Selye came into the contest with much greater visibility, political experience, and popularity. Also, his core of support was the most populous municipality in the district.

Brockport Republic publisher Horatio N. Beach pulled out all stops to support Hart. He had founded his newspaper for the express purpose of serving the Republican Party and was the secretary of the local Republican convention. He published a resolution listing 326 Republicans in Sweden and Hamlin who "pledge to you [Hart] our hearty and undivided support." They included most political and business leaders in the communities. In contrast, Beach alleged that the Rochester Democrat could cite only three names of Sweden residents who supported Selye.

Beach claimed that "ninety-nine one hundredths of the loyal people here are in favor of your return." He also made clear Hart's support for the Radicals in their clash with Johnson, saying: "We believe the false policy of Andrew Johnson can be best defeated by returning the true members of the 29th Congress." According to the *Republic*, "Johnsonites" (Democrats and Conservative Republicans) had sought the Republican nomination for Selye, including bribes "offered as high as $500" to Republican caucus members. When that failed, they persuaded him to run as an independent with the understanding that no Democrat would oppose him.

Beach published a rumor "That Mr. Selye and Miss Butler had been criminally intimate and the young lady had become the mother of a pair of twins, of which Lewis Selye was the father," adding that "we discredit the report." He also called Selye the "dupe" of the Democrats and predicted that he would be "badly defeated."

Despite Beach's predictions, Selye won by a 2,000-vote margin. Hart's margin in the Town of Sweden fell from sixty-nine in 1864 to twenty-seven. As the secret ballot had not yet been invented, the names of twenty-one Sweden Republicans who defected to Selye were well known. The *Republic* said that they had now "been blackguarded by the Democrats and distrusted by the Republicans."

In Congress, Selye was a loyal supporter of the president, but did not seek re-election in 1868. Upon retiring from Congress, he founded the *Rochester Daily*

Chronicle, which was acquired in 1870 by the *Rochester Daily Democrat* in a merger carried out by Brockport native Nathan P. Pond. That newspaper became the *Rochester Democrat & Chronicle* that we know today.

I have cribbed this essay from James Cornes's reminiscences, somewhat abridged.

Susan B. Anthony

Susan B. Anthony, the most prominent advocate of women's suffrage in the late nineteenth century, spoke publicly in Brockport at least three times. On her first visit in April 1867, Elizabeth Cady Stanton accompanied her. The *Brockport Republic* commented that "Miss Anthony is a fair speaker," but that "Mrs. Stanton is a very fine speaker, who deals in sharp logic and an occasional metaphor illustrative of her argument. She speaks much more smoothly and apparently with much greater ease than Miss Anthony."

Anthony's second visit in March 1873 received much less notice in the *Republic*. It simply said that she had drawn an audience of "about sixty" and that "Her theme was the elective franchise for women, which subject she handled with a considerable degree of skill."

Her third visit in November 1884 was a fundraiser for the Free Reading Room with an admission charge of 35 cents. The *Republic* devoted some twenty-five column inches of text to its report on the event, at which Anthony spoke for an hour and a half to a "fair-sized audience ... upon the subject: 'Women Want Bread, Not the Ballot.... The subject, however, was delusive," he said, "for the whole drift of her remarks were in advocation of woman's enfranchisement."

The reporter speculated that she had chosen the "delusive" title "in the belief that it would draw more listeners, who would expect something new, instead of the argument ... with which the majority of her hearers were previously familiar." The gist of her lecture was that the various ways in which women were treated unequally, especially "inequality of their wages as compared with men's would disappear in the twinkling of an eye" if women were granted the franchise.

The reporter called Anthony "quite a pleasant speaker, using about the same style as do other ladies who address the public ... and although she now and then hesitated a little it was evidently for the reason that it was difficult for her to select from her fund of knowledge the best facts to present. The consequence was ... that her remarks were of a rather rambling nature."

He concluded his account with the complaint that "While ... she spoke of the press ... in a very disrespectful manner, at the end she found fault because it did not take more notice of the women's movement, indicating that assistance in the good work of securing women's rights, even from this disreputable source, would be acceptable."

Frederick Douglass

Frederick Douglass, the great African-American orator, writer, and activist, was well and favorably known in Brockport. In noting his death in 1895, the *Brockport Republic* commented that he had "lectured on occasion before the Brockport Union Agricultural Society. When here he stopped with the family of Mr. A. J. Barrier. He was also a friend of Mr. and Mrs. T. A. White, who attended his funeral services at Rochester on Tuesday." Brockporters were kept apprised of his life and career by frequent mentions in the *Republic.*

I have been unable to find any accounts of Douglass's talks at the fair. However, the *Republic* did report two other lectures he delivered in Brockport. In December 1856, it reported that he had "addressed a large and highly intelligent audience in Concert Hall." The *Republic* commented that he had spoken of the "abuses and oppressions" of slavery "with a knowledge that cannot be questioned."

This was after Douglass had embraced the concept of the U.S. Constitution as an anti-slavery document. Indeed, he had argued in Brockport "that no relation exists between the U. S. Constitution and Slavery—consequently, that Slavery is unconstitutional." The *Republic* said his "masterly argument, as deduced by him from law, logic, and humanity, was listened to with deep attention by the audience."

Douglass's lecture seems to have been one of fifteen sponsored by an "Association" that included Horace Greeley; Cassius Clay, the Kentucky political leader and abolitionist; and Thomas Hart Benton, the Missouri Senator and architect of "Manifest Destiny."

It seems that Douglass did not visit Brockport again—at least, the *Republic* did not report any return. However, it continued to follow Douglass's career and kept its readers posted. It consistently expressed sympathy and support for him and for racial tolerance. For instance, in 1867, it commented "The people are advancing" when it reported that a white man had shared a seat with Douglass in a railroad car.

While Douglass resided in Rochester, he was heavily involved in Republican Party politics. In 1866, the *Republic* reported that the Democratic newspaper, the *Rochester Union*, was supporting Douglass for Congress, despite him being a Republican. In 1867, he was defeated for delegate at large for the Senatorial district convention, 86–44 votes. In 1868, the *Republic* called Douglass eminently fit for "the office of Member of Congress" and that he "would make an abler and honester Representative than we have had for the last twelve years" but that he was not "our first choice."

The *Republic* commended the National Convention of Printers in 1869 when it "Resolved, That it will be flagrantly unjust for any subordinate Union to deny admission to any printer merely on the ground of race or color." Also, it praised Douglass for saying in a speech in Albion in 1870 that there can be "no peace while oppression exists." In 1871, Douglass was defeated for member of Assembly, 5,436–4,250. However, the Republicans put him on the list of Electoral College electors for Ulysses S. Grant.

In 1873, Douglass moved from Rochester to Washington, D.C., but the *Republic* continued to report on his career. When he was appointed marshal of the District of Columbia, the *Republic* called him "well and favorably known in this section." It commended him for favoring the end of military control of the South in 1877 and for opposing "negro migration" to the North in 1878.

When Douglass died in 1895, the *Republic* commented that "American annals furnish no more captivating illustration of a self-made man, and the career of Douglass is the most convincing argument that can be advanced for the inherent possibilities of the negro race."

African-American Brockporter Gertrude Page claimed that she had been the person who discovered Douglass's body when he collapsed and died in the front hallway of his Washington home. The most recent Douglass biographer says otherwise: "Helen Douglass [Frederick's wife] was at his side, alone."

Urban Renewal

Brockport's flirtation with urban renewal began with a public meeting on December 18, 1963, attended by about forty Brockporters at which "Mr. Bibby from the State Division of Housing" presented a preliminary survey of the village showing a possible site for an urban renewal project. He advocated "total demolition of all buildings" from Park Avenue to Queen Street and from the canal to the State–Erie Streets corridor, except the Strand Theater, the Methodist Church, and the post office. If the Methodists wished, their structure could be included. Structures west of Queen Street "that tend to have a depreciating effect on the surrounding real estate" would also be removed.

Bibby told the meeting that the village board had full authority to undertake the project after "several hearings" but "without a general referendum." All costs would be borne by the state and federal governments, except that the village would be responsible for "not over $146,000" that "might be reduced to zero" if the village received funds from "the acquisition of real estate for the state college expansion."

Owners might buy back their cleared land or it could be "offered to others, including commercial land developers." "A show of hands at the end of the meeting indicated that the group present" favored further exploration of the proposal.

Another state official met with the village board in January 1964 and reported that they could expect no funds from the college expansion. He added to the project "all the land between Clinton St. and the canal as far west as the Smith St. bridge." The project would cover 22.85 acres and include 106 business structures of which seventy-eight were said to have "deficiencies," including forty-eight that were "substandard." Of the seventy-five dwelling units in the area, fifty-five were "deficient." The estimated cost was $2,435,777.

The board authorized the state to apply for funding for a "preliminary survey" and to hire an "experienced director." In March, the board published a long letter, detailing all the steps in the process of carrying through the project. It ended by reassuring Brockporters that urban renewal would not "be forced on the People of Brockport without their having a voice in it."

Mayor George Hamil was seen as the main supporter of the proposal with Trustee George Marks's active support and the "passive" acquiescence of Trustees Willis Knapp and Ellery Cooney. Trustee Don Rogers's position was seen as a mystery. In the March 1964 elections, incumbents Knapp and Cooney were defeated by Mrs. Thomas Kaznowski and Edward Grygiel. She was the first woman ever to run for a trusteeship. The winners "stressed that the voters should be well informed on urban renewal and that it should be submitted to a referendum," but were widely believed to oppose the project.

To pave the way for the project, the village board requested the state legislature to adopt a law authorizing the village to set up an urban renewal agency. However, before the legislature acted on that request, candidates opposed to the project were elected to the board in the March 1965 elections. Frank L. Sacheli (491 votes) defeated George Hamil (431) and Joseph Keable (517), and Eugene Young (490) beat incumbents Marks (447) and Harold Ehmann (401). After the election, the state assembly passed the enabling bill, but the new village board voted 3–2 to rescind the message requesting the bill and "decide at a later date whether to request the bill next year." The newly elected members favored the resolution. Kaznowski and Grygiel opposed it. Everyone talked at that time as though the project would continue to be studied. None of the elected officials opposed it openly.

In March 1967, Mayor Sacheli proposed a much more modest urban renewal project. It would provide downtown parking, beautify the canal area, and rehabilitate some of the downtown area. After an executive session, the board announced that "it had decided against seeking urban renewal funds at this time." That was the end of urban renewal for Brockport.

12

Organizations and Groups

The Grange

Brockport Grange No. 93 was probably the largest and most active local organization for some eighty years. Its membership roster often listed nearly 500 members and it held regular meetings weekly or biweekly throughout that period. It was the only organization that, for many years, had a regular front page item in the *Republic.* Also, the *Republic* frequently published news releases from the National Grange.

No. 93 was a local branch of the National Grange of the Order of Patrons of Agriculture, which described itself as "a family, community organization with its roots in agriculture." In the midst of the economic depression of the 1930s, the National Grange declared that "an important part of its mission [is] to drive away gloom, build up hope and stimulate courage, among its members." The national organization was founded in 1867 and the Brockport branch began in 1874.

Frank Capen was the founder and first "Worthy Master" of Brockport's Grange. He was a prominent farmer, and proprietor of a farm implement store. It first met in the Odd Fellows Hall, but when Capen built his "block" in 1881, it moved there. In 1911, it bought the large one-story, white structure on King Street that had been the Free Will Baptist Church and moved there. In 1929, they bought a property on Erie Street near Main Street and demolished a house on it, but they never built on it and sold it to the village for a parking lot in 1931. In 1937, they sold the King Street structure, bought the Thomas Gordon property on the corner of North Main Street and West Avenue, and converted it into a Grange Hall. In 1946, they sold that property and met in the Clarkson Town Hall or, occasionally, in a member's home.

Most Grange regular meetings began with a "tureen dinner," followed by a business meeting. Much of the business meetings was taken up with promotions of members from one "degree" to a higher one. Meetings concluded with some sort of "program." Programs included a great variety of activities, lectures, debates, musical programs, a minstrel show, picnics, spelling bees, Christmas, Valentines, and Hallowe'en parties, Memorial Day observances, Flower Shows, card parties, ballroom and barn dances, strawberry and ice cream socials, dinners, wiener roasts, baked food sales, fairs, etc. From time-to-time, they had a "Neighbor Night" hosting a nearby Grange or a "Booster Night," an outreach event, inviting non-members in the community to join them.

Performing plays was one of their most popular activities. They even formed an orchestra at one time and had an "Athletic Club" or a "Juvenile Grange" for their youth. Though they claimed nearly 500 members at times and as many as 300 attended their annual picnic, meeting attendance rarely exceeded 100. In 1929, for instance, they claimed 463 members, but only "about 80" attended one of the September meetings. Thus, it may be that many members joined only for the inexpensive fire insurance on farm buildings that it offered and were not really active in the organization. As late as 1955, the Brockport Grange claimed about 250 members and met bimonthly.

Meetings included talks by professional agricultural experts such as professors from the School of Agriculture at Cornell and specialists from the Agricultural Extension Service at Geneva. The Grange, both locally and nationally, often took positions on public policy issues, especially those that affected agriculture. Positions taken by the Brockport Grange included opposing daylight savings time for Brockport and supporting a gasoline tax.

The Grange boasted that women were treated as equal from the beginning and played an active role in the organization. Women frequently presented programs for the meetings. For instance, in 1925, one of the meetings was designated "Canning Night" and women were invited to bring home-canned items and discuss the process that produced them. About half of the officers of the local Grange were women, though none of the "Worthy Masters" seems to have been a woman.

The Grange continued to meet at the Clarkson Town Hall, though it got much less attention from the *Republic*—and the frequency of those meetings is not known—until it dissolved sometime around 1970. The state headquarters of the Grange has not been able to tell me when it dissolved.

The Nazarites

The Nazarites were a religious sect that began in Brockport and became a Protestant religious denomination. An essay above recounts the career of Benjamin Titus Roberts, who started the sect and later founded the denomination, the Free Methodists. He had been the pastor in Brockport's Methodist Church, 1853–55.

The *Brockport Republic* of December 19, 1856, reported that the "Nazarites" was "a new sect that has originated in the Methodist society in this village. A considerable ill feeling has for some time existed between them and the main body of the society, from which we learn they are about to withdraw." They had held two "largely attended" meetings in the former Free Will Baptist Church on King Street. The *Republic* reported that the "only difference between them and the regular Methodists ... is their mode of worship and *perfection* in worldly life."

The *Republic* of December 26 published a resolution of "the Quarterly Conference, at Brockport Station, Genesee Conference, Nov. 29, 1856," declaring that "we regard the 'Nazarite'" movement as factious, turbulent, contrary to the true spirit of Christianity and dangerous to the highest interests of the Church of God" and asking "the Trustees of this Church not ... allow any [Nazarite] minister to occupy the pulpit."

A letter to the editor from a "Methodist" in the January 2, 1857, issue of the *Republic* denied that the Nazarites were a new sect, but rather were "some of the oldest, most pious members of the church" and practiced their religion "particularly as taught by one John Wesley." In short, they believed that the main church had departed from Wesley's teachings and that they were returning to them. It also denied that the Nazarites were "withdrawing" from the main church, but were being "driven out by the high handed power of the other portion."

Three weeks later, the *Republic* published a response from "Member" to that letter. It argued that the Nazarites had not been refused permission to meet in the church, but had failed to avail themselves of the procedures for applying for that permission. It also denied that the Nazarites were being "driven out" of the church, rather "there is a disposition to be kind and lenient toward those who are believed to be in error—hoping thereby that they may be convinced of it—and that the unhappy division which has lately so embarrassed the church may thus be removed."

The debate continued in the pages of the *Republic* for several more weeks and was eventually resolved when Roberts led his followers out of the mainstream Methodist denomination and founded the Free Methodist denomination. Several members of the Brockport church followed him into the new denomination.

African-Americans in the Town of Sweden

The 1814 N.Y.S. census shows no African-Americans in the town, but by 1820, a childless black farming couple appeared and were still here in 1830. The 1825 state census registered nine "colored" residents, but that figure dropped to six by 1830. They included a couple and their small daughter. The husband, John Johnson, was a barber, a common trade for African-Americans in the nineteenth century. He was the first of some twenty-one African-American men who practiced—and practically dominated—that trade here.

The best known of the barbers was Anthony J. Barrier, who barbered in Brockport from his arrival in 1829 at the age of fifteen until his death in his shop in 1890, sixty-one years later. He was a prominent and respected member of the political, business, and religious community and the father of civil rights leader Fannie Barrier Williams. He was treasurer of the Baptist Church for ten years and his wife, Harriet, was a Sunday school teacher. His brother-in-law, Troy A. White, also had a barber shop in Brockport then. The Barriers were a Brockport family from 1829 until Anthony's daughter, Ella, died here in 1946.

The largest number of blacks in Brockport in any census between 1814 and 1925 was fifty-three in 1875. After that, the number declined steadily until only Gertrude and Harry Page remained in 1920. A total of 187 black people lived in Brockport at one time or another during that period. Occupationally, the men were distributed fairly equally between lower middle-class trades, thirty-two, and common laborer, twenty-two. Most of the women, twenty-four, were employed in domestic service, but seven were seamstresses, two were hairdressers, and twenty-six were not employed outside the home. Three Brockport African-Americans served in the Union Army, two of them in white regiments.

Aside from the white families that employed black residents as domestic servants or farmhands, there were a number of biracial households. A black farmer and farrier housed three young white men in 1840 and eight in 1850. Another had two white children and a white woman in his household and still another housed a white woman and child. Also, there were three cases of black men married to white women and one white man wed to a black woman.

According to the censuses, no slave ever lived in the town, and, apparently, very few former slaves did so either. Most intriguing was the household of William H. Seymour, Brockport's most distinguished citizen. The 1855 census reported that a young "Black" woman, not identified as a servant, resided in his household. In the 1865 census, he housed a black servant and two black teenagers and, in 1870, a ten-year-old boy, all born in Virginia, so apparently they had been born slaves.

Seven black people on the 1875 census had been born in southern states and probably had been slaves. The most notable of the former slaves was William L. Page; he had been born a slave in Key West, Florida, in 1834, and arrived in

Brockport about 1870. He was a graduate of Macedon Academy and claimed to have been the first African-American graduate of the University of Rochester, though the school has no record of his attendance. He was an engineer on the Erie Canal and partnered with Anthony Barrier in the coal business for three years in the 1870s.

During their first century in the Town of Sweden, African-Americans were a continuous and, sometimes, important presence, but never formed more than a small percentage of the population. Perhaps because of the small numbers, they seem to have been thoroughly integrated into the life of the community.

13

Some Overviews

A Year in Review

A feature much favored by American newspapers for the end of a calendar year is a review of the top news stories of the past twelve months. The *Brockport Republic* was no exception. So this essay takes a look at what Brockporters of 1915 were told were the top news stories of the previous year.

The biggest news event of 1914 was the war in Europe. The *Republic* listed ninety-five newsworthy events in the conflagration from July 23 until November 13. A Western Hemisphere war also got some attention. Mexico was torn apart by a civil war and the United States posted troops in the city of Vera Cruz from April 11 until November 23. Ironically, the *Republic* also noted two items reporting American peace treaties with eighteen foreign countries, including Great Britain and France, but not Germany, the Ottoman Empire, or Austro-Hungary.

Besides war and peace, the *Republic* reported on other significant events: the Federal Reserve banks began operations, and it remains the foundation of our public finance system; canal business was booming, and the Panama and Cape Cod Canals opened; the Kiel Canal reopened, and the U.S. and Nicaragua signed a treaty for the U.S. to build a canal across that country; Great Britain granted Home Rule to Ireland; and President Wilson's wife died and his daughter got married.

In sports, the Boston Nationals beat the American Athletics in the World Series, and Harvard had a good year, beating Yale 36–0 in football and winning the Henley Regatta in England. To further humiliate the English, an American horse won at Epsom Downs.

Though the *Republic* reminded its readers of those events and many more, it had not reported them when they happened—the list came from a syndicate. It also did not publish a review of local events, but if it had, it might have included these items: Father Story died after fifty-one years as priest at Nativity; Brockport got a new water system, drawing water from Lake Ontario; natural gas was being piped in; a Grammar School replaced the three district schools; and a town clock, still keeping time in the Methodist Church tower, was installed. Additionally, three new industries appeared: the Rochester Wheel Works plant was converted to the Brockport Cold Storage plant; the Brockport Fruit Growers Assn. opened another cold storage plant at 1 Park Avenue; and the Monitor Clock Co. replaced the former Phelps Piano Case Co. One of its products is ticking away at this moment in my front hall. On the other hand, the Louisman-Capen Piano Co. went bankrupt. A. D. Daily died and left to his son-in-law, A. V. Fowler, the funeral home he had founded in 1868 that is still in business.

The village board adopted a $43,000 annual budget, less than 1 percent of our current budget. The Normal School had the largest graduating class in history, 101 students, and Brockport's Monroe County Fair had the largest attendance ever and was favored by an appearance by Governor Glynn.

So, as we look back at 1914, we see that our legacy from those Brockporters includes a cold storage plant, a clock in my home and one in the church tower, a water system, natural gas, and the oldest business in town, and although the Grammar School was replaced by the Barclay School in 1956, its demise made room for the village's most popular playground. A pretty good record for one year.

Village Trustees, 1866–1916

Presidents

1866 Thomas Cornes
1867 Thomas Cornes
1868 Thomas Cornes
1869 Dayton S. Morgan
1870 Josiah Harrison
1871 Josiah Harrison
1872 Luther Gordon
1873 John H. Kingsbury
1874 Myrick O. Randall
1875 James Cotter, Jr.
1876 Myron M. Oliver
1877 Myron M. Oliver
1878 George T. Cornes
1879 George T. Cornes
1880 John H. Kingsbury
1881 George R. Ward
1882 George R. Ward
1883 John H. Kingsbury
1884 John H. Kingsbury
1885 John H. Kingsbury
1886 George R. Ward
1887 George R. Ward
1888 George R. Ward
1889 Franklin F. Capen

1890 Franklin F. Capen
1891 Franklin F. Capen
1892 Franklin F. Capen
1893 Charles H. Philbrook
1894 Benjamin F. Gleason
1895 Thomas H. Dobson
1896 George L. Lovejoy
1897 George L. Lovejoy
1898 James Brennan
1899 Philip F. Swart
1900 Philip F. Swart
1901 Delbert A. Adams
1902 John W. Cunningham
1903 Benjamin F. Gleason
1904 Charles E. Shafer
1905 Alfred M. White
1906 James W. Larkin
1907 James W. Larkin
1908 William W. Guelph
1909 Lewis W. Udell
1910 Lewis W. Udell
1911 Luther G. Gordon
1912 Luther G. Gordon
1913 Luther G. Gordon
1914 George B. Harmon
1915 George B. Harmon
1916 George B. Harmon

Trustees

Lafayette Silliman 1866–1867
Edgar Benedict 1866–1868
Sydney Spaulding 1866
Henry W. Seymour 1866–1868
Lucius T. Underhill 1867–1868
Edward Harrison 1868, 1880, 1882, 1899, 1905
William Bradford 1869
Aaron N. Bramin 1869
John Owens 1869, 1871
Thomas C. Berry 1869, 1875, 1880
Edgar Brown 1870–1874, 1877–1880
Charles Benedict 1870, 1873
John Welch 1870, 1871
William H. Roberts 1870
Henry S. Wood 1871
Samuel Johnston 1872
G. H. Allen 1872
John A. Latta 1872
William G. Raines 1873
Angus G. Boyd 1874–1876
Robert J. Fellows 1874
James Cotter, Jr. 1874
Jacob A. Sleaster 1875
Ezra N. Hill 1875–1877
Daniel Paine 1876
Patrick Donellan 1876–1877, 1898
Nelson A. Smith 1877–1881, 1883, 1885
George A. Ward 1878–1879
Charles C. Cornes 1878–1879
James Bendle 1878–1879
Charles Van Eps 1880–1881
Homer M. Johnston 1881
Henry W. Cary 1881
Daniel Pease 1882
William Welch 1882
Herman Buckingham 1883
John Allen 1883
Horace Belden 1884
James Berry 1884, 1887
John Flynn 1884
George T. Cornes 1885
Henry S. Madden 1886, 1888
Charles W. Root 1886
Frank E. Velzey 1886

Thomas H. Dobson 1887, 1905
Addison Palmer 1887
Delbert A. Adams 1887
Charles W. Root 1888, 1893
George A. Williams 1888
Raphael J. Cook 1889, 1891
John W. Cunningham 1889, 1893–1894, 1896
Benjamin F. Gleason 1889, 1892
Thomas C. Berry 1889, 1892, 1902, 1904
Adolph May 1889–1890, 1892
John R. Davis 1891
Arthur W. Fowler 1893, 1895
Robert Currie 1893–1894
William H. Burns 1894
Philip F. Swart 1895, 1898
Philetus P. Moore 1896
George A. Nichols 1896, 1898–1899
James Brennan 1897
Frank A. Bonnell 1898
Julius Heinrich 1898, 1900, 1902
C.P. Lane 1898
James R. Elliott 1899
Silas Holbrook 1899
Luther Gordon 1900, 1902, 1904, 1910
Emery J. Le Barron 1900, 1906
Frank W. Consaul 1900
Addison Palmer 1900–1901
John F. Dailey 1901
William R. Blossom 1901
Charles E. Shafer 1903
Arthur G. Coleman 1903
George E. Locke 1903
Rolland A. Chandler 1904, 1906
Alfred M. White 1904
Harris Holmes 1905
G. Fred Clark 1906–1908
Frank D. Hebbard 1907, 1909, 1912
Lewis W. Udell 1907
George C. Brown 1907, 1909, 1911, 1913, 1915
George A. Whitney 1908, 1910
Roswell L. Chase 1908
Maurice P. Crotty 1909, 1911, 1913
John T. Wilson 1910, 1912
Frank G. Gleason 1911
Frank B. Miller 1911–1912
Frank G. Curwin 1913
Thomas C. Gordon 1914, 1916
Warren B. Conkling 1914, 1916
John H. Welch 1914, 1916
Alfred C. Thompson 1915
Herbert W. Bramley 1915

Elective offices

Clerk 1866–1872
Treasurer 1866–1916
Street Commissioner 1866–1872
Assessors 1866–1916
Collector 1866–1914
Police Constable 1866–1872
Pound Keeper 1866–1872
Police Justice 1867–1871, 1895
John R. Davis, Treasurer 1894–1912

Life in Brockport is Transformed in Fifty Years

Life for Brockporters changed dramatically between 1866, the first year after the Civil War, and 1916, the last year before American entry in World War I. The example of the life of a member of the community who lived as an adult throughout that period will illustrate that. Daniel Holmes was Brockport's most prominent lawyer and a civic leader.

Daniel Holmes was thirty-seven years old as 1866 began and a very old, retired lawyer in 1916. He was the longtime village clerk and secretary of the Normal School board, among many other things. Thus, he lived through the fifty-year transformation of the village. To illustrate the changes that occurred and the impact they had on the lives of Brockporters, I will describe his life, first in 1866 and then in 1916.

Upon arising each morning, Holmes fetched fuel and built a fire in a coal range and drew water from a well in the backyard or from a cistern in the basement to heat water to wash up and shave and for his breakfast needs. Occasionally, the well would be dry. Before leaving for his office, he tended to his horse, fed it oats and hay, carried a bucket of water, cleaned the stall, and brushed down the horse.

Holmes lived on College Street and his law office was on Main Street downtown. To get back and forth, he walked on wooden sidewalks. He had to walk carefully, because the walks were uneven. Each property owner built his portion of the walk at his expense according to specifications set by the village board. Property owners who failed to meet the deadline set by the board or varied from its specifications were fined. The sidewalk sections did not always align properly. Nails sometimes stuck out to pierce the unwary foot. Holmes needed to watch out for broken and missing boards. Heavy rains might wash away whole sections. The village lost several lawsuits because of the poor condition of the walks.

On his way, Holmes walked across four dirt streets that were dusty in dry weather and muddy in wet. He stepped carefully to avoid the horse manure and watched out for the occasional runaway horse, an accident that happened more frequently then than auto collisions do today.

At his office, Holmes tended a small coal stove to keep warm. He had no air conditioning on hot summer days. He had a kerosene lamp for illumination, and he needed to refill the kerosene tank each day, lift the glass to adjust the wick, and light the wick. If the wick was not properly adjusted, the lamp smoked up the office.

If Holmes needed to communicate with a client, he wrote a note, delivered it on foot to the post office, and retrieved the day's mail. He timed that errand to coincide with the arrival of the day's mail from the central post office in Rochester. Alternatively, he might go on foot to deliver his note to the client's home or place of employment. Personal communications required similar effort.

Back home in the evening, Holmes's routine suffered the same complications as it did in the morning. In addition, he carried the ash tray from his coal stove to the ash pit in the backyard to empty it. When he needed to relieve himself, he would retreat to a backyard privy, whether from discomfort at night, in a raging blizzard, or on a hot, stuffy day.

On Election Day, Holmes brought to the polling site a ballot printed up by his preferred candidates and cast it in full view of his neighbors, as the secret ballot did not yet exist. Incidentally, the lack of a secret ballot and the general political subservience of women meant that women's suffrage would have given married men two votes, whereas single men would have had only one. To travel to Rochester, Buffalo, or points in between, he went by horse and buggy or the New York Central Railroad that had reached Brockport only fourteen years earlier. It meant a day's excursion by buggy to Rochester or two days to Buffalo. If he went by rail, he needed public transportation to go from the depot to his destination.

If his house caught fire, he would mobilize his neighbors to form a bucket brigade, because the village's fire company had ceased to function.

The children of his neighbors attended the elementary grades in a district schoolhouse where the Monika Andrews Children's Park is now, one of three in the village. The six grades in each school were taught by two teachers in two rooms, with no indoor plumbing, air conditioning, or central heating. The Brockport Collegiate Institute that had provided secondary education for village children had gone bankrupt three years earlier and the building had been sold at foreclosure sale for $365.

Now, let us turn our time machine ahead fifty years. By 1916, eighty-seven-year-old Holmes illuminated his home and office by flipping switches. He drew hot and cold water by opening spigots. Wells and cisterns fell into disuse. Electric stoves and hot water heaters were available. Flush toilets connected to a municipal sanitary sewer had replaced privies. The concrete sidewalks were much more even, free of dangerous nails and missing pieces, and never floated away. The streets were hard-surfaced, no mud, no dust, much less horse manure. Bicycles and automobiles replaced most horses. Telephones and home and office mail delivery facilitated communications.

By 1916, voting machines had been introduced, permitting the secret ballot. Holmes could travel by automobile on his own schedule without resorting to public transportation at his destination. Alternatively, he could use the inter-city trolley and the N.Y.C.R.R. was still available. Finally, he had fire protection from Brockport's first municipal fire department.

In 1866, Holmes had already served for twelve years as secretary to the board of the Brockport Collegiate Institute, which had constantly been on the brink of bankruptcy. In 1916, he was nearing a half century of service as the secretary to the board of the Brockport State Normal School, a solid, state-funded institution of higher education, housed in a much-enlarged structure that provided free secondary education for the village children.

Holmes's neighbors' children now attended a Grammar School with all the elementary-level students of the village. Each grade was in a separate room taught by its own dedicated teacher. They now had indoor plumbing, electric lighting, and central heating.

The Barge Canal with mechanical power had replaced Clinton's Ditch with its animal power. The steep, wooden high bridges on Main Street and Park Avenue that had caused so many accidents had been replaced by the modern, steel lift bridges that still serve.

Thus, Holmes in 1866 lived very much the way his ancestors had lived several generations earlier. By 1916, his life was not that much different from ours today. The transformation was probably more radical than at any other similar period in history.

Brockport Timeline

The timeline below identifies some of the key events in the history of Brockport. Brockport's history before 1856 is a bit sketchy because the village records burned in a fire in 1856 and few issues of newspapers before the founding of the *Brockport Republic* in 1856 have survived.

1791: Massachusetts cedes Triangular Tract to Robert Morris.
1793: Leroy, Bayard, McEvers, and Clarkson acquire Triangular Tract.
1797: Senecas cede interest in Triangular Tract.
1802: Lake Road laid out from Leroy to Lake Ontario.
1804: William Peters is first settler in the Brockport area.
1808: Edward Parks is first settler where Brockport is now.
1813: Town of Sweden created.
1817: James Seymour opens store in Clarkson. Hiel Brockway family settles where Brockport is now.
1821: Seymour and associates buy land where Brockport is now.
1822: Brockport streets are laid out. Seymour becomes first Monroe County Sheriff.
1823: Erie Canal reaches Brockport.
1825: Completed canal opens.
1827: *Brockport Free Press* weekly newspaper founded.
1828: Brockway founds Red Bird packet line. Methodists build first church in Brockport on Market Street. Baptists build a church a month later on Main Street
1829: Brockport receives its charter as a village. Brockport Temperance Society formed.

1830: Brockport Baptist College authorized. Brockport's population is 798. First "real" schoolhouse opens. Presbyterians build a church on State Street.
1833: *Brockport Free Press* ceases publication.
1838: First Brockport bank opens.
1841: Brockport Collegiate Institute founded.
1844: Brockporter Elias B. Holmes elected to U.S. Congress.
1845: Free Will Baptists build a church on King Street.
1846: *Brockport Watchman* semi-weekly newspaper founded.
1851: Catholics begin to build a church on Erie Street.
1853: Brockporter Davis Carpenter elected to U.S. Congress.
1854: Brockport Collegiate Institute building burns.
1855: Fannie Barrier, future civil rights leader is born. Benjamin Titus Roberts preaches to "Nazarites," eventually Free Methodists. St. Luke's Episcopal Church built on Main Street. Brockport Collegiate Institute re-opens in new building.
1856: Horatio N. Beach founds the *Brockport Republic* weekly newspaper. John Owens opens grocery store on Main and Clinton Streets. Luther Gordon arrives in Brockport, founds lumber business.
1857: John Ostrom completes building the Morgan-Manning House. First Brockport Agricultural Fair.
1858: Edward Harrison becomes merchant tailor in Brockport.
1859: Gas lighting begins in Brockport.
1860: Town of Sweden votes for Lincoln, 571–264.
1861: Two Union Army companies were recruited In Brockport.
1862: Four Union Army companies were recruited in Brockport. Evangelical Reformed Lutheran church built on Monroe Avenue.
1863: Luther Gordon founds the First National Bank of Brockport. First Baptist Church built on Main Street.
1866: Former Congressman Elias B. Holmes dies at fifty-nine.
1867: Brockport State Normal School was founded.
1868: Byron Huntley and Samuel Johnston found Johnston Harvester Co.
1870: Fannie Barrier is first African-American graduate of Normal School. *Brockport Democrat* weekly newspaper founded.
1874: Brockport Fire Department founded.
1876: Thomas Dobson opens drugstore in Brockport. Brockport Methodist Church built on Main Street.
1877: Seymour & Morgan foundry becomes D.S. Morgan & Co. Fire destroys many Market Street buildings.
1878: Wilson H. Moore founds Moore Subscription Agency.
1880: First bicycle appears in Brockport.
1881: First telephones arrive in Brockport.

1882: Johnston Harvester Co. factory burns.
1883: Julius Lester opens dry goods store on Market Street.
1884: Village hall and fire station built on Market Street.
1886: Whiteside, Barnett & Co. farm implement firm is dissolved.
1887: First German Evangelical Lutheran Concordia Church built on Spring Street.
1888: Electrical lighting system begins operation in Brockport. Moore-Shafer Shoe Manufacturing Co. formed.
1890: Dayton S. Morgan dies and company is soon dissolved.
1893: Julius Lester moves his dry goods store to Main and King Streets.
1894: Brockport Piano Manufacturing Co. founded.
1897: Rochester Wheel Co. occupies D.S. Morgan & Co.'s Plant No. 2.
1899: Home delivery of the mail begins in Brockport.
1900: Wilson H. Moore is first Brockporter to own an automobile.
1902: Former Congressman Richard C. Shannon buys home at Main and College Streets.
1903: Brockport's municipal sewer system begins operation. William H. Seymour dies at the age of 101.
1904: Brockport Yacht Club formed.
1907: Mary Jane Holmes dies at the age of eighty-two. Wilson H. Moore shoots himself in apparent suicide.
1907: Grammar School opens on Utica Street.
1908: Inter-city trolley service begins from Rochester to Buffalo.
1908: Lyric (later Strand) Theater opens in Winslow Block.
1910: Alfred Thompson becomes Normal School Principal.
1911: Old Home Week celebrated in July.
1912: Dunn Furniture Store opens.
1913: Rochester Wheel Co. fails, plant becomes Brockport Cold Storage.
1914: Brockport's municipal water system begins operation.
1915: The Sweden section of the N.Y.S. Barge Canal is built.
1916: Edward Harrison dies and his son continues merchant tailor business.
1919: Daniel Holmes dies at the age of ninety-one.
1920: Brockport Piano Manufacturing Co. moves to East Rochester. John Owens dies after sixty-four years in the grocery business.
1924: Brockport's first hospital opens on North Main Street.
1925: The *Brockport Republic* takes over the *Brockport Democrat.*
1926: Nativity of the Blessed Virgin Mary Catholic Church built on Main Street.
1927: President Thomas Gordon builds new First National Bank building. Brockport Hospital moves to Main Street.
1929: Moore-Shafer Shoe Manufacturing Co. fails.
1930: Unemployment caused severe suffering in Brockport.

1931: Brockport Freezers are N.Y.S. Rural Baseball League champions. Inter-city trolley service ends.
1932: Brockport Freezers baseball team thirty-eight-game win streak ends. Rochester Gas & Electric Co. closes Brockport gas plant.
1933: Last Monroe County Fair held in Brockport. First National Bank of Brockport fails.
1934: Brockport High School opens in Allen street building.
1936: Seymour Public Library opens on State Street. Dog Idaho on probation for drowning death of boy. Ernest Hartwell becomes Normal School Principal.
1938: Cornerstone laid for Hartwell Hall.
1940: Brockport Post Office is built.
1942: Normal School becomes State Teachers College.
1944: Fannie Barrier Williams dies in Brockport, aged eighty-nine. Gifford Morgan dies, aged seventy. Donald Tower becomes Brockport State Teachers College president.
1948: General Electric opens small appliance manufacturing plant in Brockport.
1951: Lakeside Hospital moves to West Avenue.
1955: Allied Group formed, enters frozen food storage business in 1982. Landmark Hotel (formerly American Hotel) burns.
1956: Barclay Elementary School opens.
1961: Owens-Illinois builds glass container plant in Brockport.
1964: Fire badly damages Morgan-Manning House killing Sarah Morgan Manning. Passenger service ends on rail line in Brockport.
1965: Albert W. Brown becomes Brockport College President.
1967: Dobson Drug Store closes after ninety-one years. High School moves to new building, Middle School opens in old one. Western Monroe Historical Society formed.
1969: Market Street Village Hall demolished, Village moves to State Street.
1972: The *Brockport Republic-Democrat* ceases publication. Market Street firehouse opens.
1973: Jim Stull begins twenty-year service as mayor.
1981: John W. Van de Wetering becomes Brockport College president.
1982: A. & P. packing plant closes.
1984: General Electric sells its Brockport plant to Black & Decker.
1989: Kleen-Brite Laboratories buys Black & Decker plant.
1993: Maryann Thorpe becomes mayor.
1996: Seymour Public Library moves to East Avenue.
1997: Paul Yu becomes Brockport College president.
2000: Village offices move to former Seymour Library building.
2001: Kleen Brite closes its Brockport plant. Josephine Matela becomes mayor.

2002: Brockport Community Museum receives provisional charter. Greater Brockport Development Corporation organized.
2004: John Halstead becomes Brockport College president.
2005: Canalside Welcome Center opens. Mort Wechsler becomes mayor.
2006: The *Brockport Post* ceases publication.
2009: Connie Castenada becomes mayor.
2011: Lakeside Hospital closes.
2012: Margay Blackman becomes mayor. Strong West healthcare facility opens.
2014: Heidi Macpherson becomes Brockport College president.
2018: Village hall moves to 127 Main Street.

Bibliographical Note

When Margay Blackman became Brockport's mayor in 2012, and I became deputy mayor, she asked me to begin each village board meeting with a brief historical moment. I did so until I retired from the board in 2018 and presented a historical moment only once a month thereafter. As I had no thought at the time of publishing those brief essays, I kept no bibliographical information. When quite a few of those "moments" had accumulated, I came to believe that they could be brought together in book form. In preparing the book manuscript, I added material so that some of them were no longer "brief." Most of the material came from the files of the weekly *Brockport Republic*. Nearly complete files of that newspaper and its successor, the *Brockport Republic-Democrat*, are available and searchable online at nyshistoricnewspapers.org, on microfilm at several area libraries, and as bound paper volumes at Brockport's Emily Knapp Museum. I also used a few issues of the *Brockport Democrat*, available as microfilm at several area libraries. Finally, Wikipedia was sometimes helpful in filling in gaps.